教书育人

100句

[中英对照]

100 Quotations on Educating and
Fostering People

刘彭芝（LIU Pengzhi）　著

人民出版社

目 录
Catalog

自 序

刘彭芝

时光飞逝如闪电。

不知不觉中，我在基础教育一线已经工作了 54 个春秋。

无论愿意不愿意、自觉不自觉，我似乎都到了该"盘点"自己教育生涯的时候了。因此，中央文史研究馆在讨论研究年度课题时，当领导建议我将自己的讲话文章中关于教育的一些言辞整理一下，编辑出版《教书育人 100 句》时，我同意了。

从跨进中学校门开始，做数学教师，当校长，我一直是个实务工作者，总体上是个不善言辞、苦于表达的人。习近平总书记那句"伟大梦想不是等得来、喊得来的，而是拼出来、干出来的"，真是说到了我的心坎上，我相信"行胜于言"，相信"实践出真知"。在基础教育一线工作半个多世纪，这本《教书育人 100 句》，是我一路拼搏的雪泥鸿爪。

言为心声。

《教书育人 100 句》，贯穿着一个梦想，那就是办一所"国内领先，国际一流"的中学；传递着一种理念，那就是"爱与尊重"，办好学校，关键是把学生的个性和潜能发掘出来，把教师的积极性和创造性调动起来；洋溢着一股气息，那就是改革创新的时代精神。

《教书育人 100 句》几乎都是我 1997 年担任人大附中校长后讲的。需要特别说明的是，这些话与其说是对师生讲的，不如说是对我自己讲的；与其说是对师生的要求，不如说是对我自己的要求。每一句话都不是坐而论道，都不是游谈无根，其背后都是一项或多项实实在在的工作措施和行动。

感谢人大附中的陈华、徐铮、崔潞、李桦、徐华莹、张卫汾、谢鸣钟老师为此书所做的工作。

因为没有上下文，特别是没有背景介绍，《教书育人 100 句》难免单薄枯燥。感谢人大附中的两位毕业生王羽熙、杨子艺为每句话配画了意趣盎然的插图，他们的青春和才情，让本书返原了一些校园的情境和气息。

编辑出版《教书育人100句》，绝没有金针度人之意。只是觉得这些只言片语能给同事们留下较深印象，或许对其他读者也能有所启发，果能如此，幸莫大焉。

2019 年 4 月 20 日，时为谷雨

Author's Preface

Liu Pengzhi

How time flies in a blink of an eye.

Before I realised it, it has been 54 years since I started to work at the forefront of secondary education.

Whether like it or not, whether being aware or unaware, it's about time to "review" my career in education. When the Central Research Institute of Culture and History discussed annual research topics, the leader suggested that I organize and publish some of my opinions from previous speeches and articles regarding educating and fostering people, and published as 100 quotations, and I took his advice.

Ever since I stepped through the gate of high school first as a mathematics teacher and later as the principal, I have always been pragmatic. In general, finding the words to express my thoughts clearly can sometimes be a struggle but the words of Chairman Xi that goes "great dreams are not achieved through waiting around and talking, but through diligence and hard-work" have really resonated with me. I believe that "actions speak louder than words", and "practice makes perfect". After more than half a century working at the forefront of secondary education, this book *100 Quotations on Educating and Fostering People* traces my journey along the path of education and self development.

Words are the voice of the mind.

There is a dream that filters through the whole *100 Quotations on Educating and Fostering People*, which is to run a "domestically lead and internationally top class" school; there is an ideal growing which says "love and respect", and only by drawing out the positive characteristics and potential of the students, as well as stimulating the passion and innovation of the teachers that can produce an exceptionally well run school. There is an atmosphere that brims with the spirit of revolution and innovation.

The contents of *100 Quotations on Educating and Fostering People* are almost all from the period from when I became the headmaster of the High School Affiliated to Renmin University of China in 1997. What needs to be clarified is that all of these words and thoughts reflect my inner conversations of speaking to myself rather than those I had with teachers and students; they are similar to guidance for myself rather than for teachers and students. Each sentence neither just sits alone or prattles about the general principle. Behind them are actually multiple practical working measures and actions.

I would like to express my sincere gratitude to the following teachers from The High School Affiliated to Renmin University of China for all their efforts into this book: CHEN Hua, XU Zheng, CUI Lu, LI Hua, XU Huaying, ZHANG Weifen, XIE Mingzhong.

100 Quotations on Educating and Fostering People could be dull and dry without context and especially without a background introduction. I offer my thanks to WANG Yuxi, YANG Ziyi, the two graduates of The High School Affiliated to Renmin University of China who draw the charming and interesting illustrations for each quotation. Their youth and talent has brought back some of the campus feel and flavor into the book.

Editing and publishing *100 Quotations on Educating and Fostering People* was never meant to instruct others about the skills of teaching. I just think if these varied thoughts could leave my colleagues with a deep impression then they may inspire other readers. If the book connects with its readers, that would be very fortunate.

April 20th of 2019. On Grain Rain

一、人生为一大事来

1. 教育是我的人生大事
2. 教育让我的人生充盈而幸福
3. 我的理想是办一所让世人向往的学校
4. 教育是事业
5. 做一名兼具"中国情怀、世界视野"的
   当代中国教育家
6. 教育是一切

I. We All Live for an Aspiration

1. Education is my aspiration
2. Education makes my life full and happy
3. My dream is to open a school that people greatly desire
4. Education is an undertaking
5. Be an educationist in contemporary China with "Chinese
   feelings and global vision"
6. Education is everything

1. 教育是我的人生大事

　　我来到世上，所为的大事是什么？做教师时，我的人生大事是做一名好教师；当校长时，我的人生大事是当一名好校长。教育，是我的人生大事；爱，是我在教育岗位上进德修业的原动力。我的青春，我的全部心血，都献给了我的人生大事。

1. Education is my aspiration

　　What is the aspiration that I bring to this world? As a teacher, my life's aspiration was to be a good teacher and as a principal, it was also my aspiration to be an excellent principal. Education is the goal of my life, and love has been the original motivation for me as I progressed through my working life in education. My youth and all of my painstaking efforts, have been dedicated to this life's aim.

2. 教育让我的人生充盈而幸福

孟子讲，人生有三大"至乐"：一是父母俱存，兄弟无故；二是仰不愧于天，俯不怍于人；三是得天下英才而教育之。这三大"至乐"我曾全部享受过，我的人生是快乐的。我是一个幸福的人。

2. Education makes my life full and happy

Mencius said that people have three "extreme blessings": the first is both parents are alive and your brothers suffer no illnesses and resentment. The second is that one has nothing to feel guilty for, and is not ashamed of anything when he faces people. The third is one can gather talented people together and has the opportunity to nurture them. I have enjoyed all of these three "extreme blessings", so my life is filled with bliss, and I am a happy human being.

3. 我的理想是办一所让世人向往的学校

　　我的理想是办一所中国的世界顶级学校，一所让世人仰慕向往的学校。它不仅吸引中国的孩子，而且能吸引世界各地的孩子到这里学习。我希望孩子们离开学校回忆起自己的中学时代感觉是幸福快乐的，是有独特收获的；我希望人大附中的校园成为孩子们最向往、最喜欢、最留恋的地方。

3. My dream is to open a school that people greatly desire

My dream is to open a world-class school in China, a school that everyone respects and of which everyone wants to be a part. It will not only attract children from China, but also students from all over the world who will aspire to come and study here. I hope when the children reminisce about their high school time after leaving it, they would feel happy and cheerful, and would remember it as a rewarding part of their lives. I hope the campus of The High School Affiliated to Renmin University of China would become the most yearned for, admired, and a place of warmest memories for the students.

有这样一所学校
——中外教育者
眼中的人大附中

4. 教育是事业

人为万物之灵，世界上还有什么工作能比培养人的工作更重要、更伟大？仅凭这一点，我们就不能单纯视教育为职业。志小则易足，易足则无由进，立大志才能办大事。教育工作者要立大志办大事，必须将教育作为事业。将教育作为事业，才能有强烈的事业心，崇高的使命感；才能视教育如生命，视学校如家庭，视学生如子弟；才能朝夕虑其事，日夜经其务，无私奉献，鞠躬尽瘁；才能拒绝平庸，追求卓越，以第一等的正气、第一等的襟怀、第一等的追求，臻于第一等的境界，取得第一等的业绩。

4. Education is an undertaking

Human beings are the highest form of all creatures. What other work in the world can be more important and mighty than the cause of educating people? If only for this purpose, we should not consider education merely as a job. It's easy to satisfy a small wish, thus there shall be no reason to make more progress; one can only make great advancements with great aspirations. Educators should cherish high aspirations to achieve these accomplishments. Only by treating education as an undertaking, shall we have the strong dedication and a high sense of mission. We could see education as our lives, our school as our family, and our students as our own children. We should put this to the forefront of our minds from morning to evening, work on it day and night, devote ourselves to it selflessly and strive to our utmost ability for it. We should refuse to be ordinary, in order to pursue excellence. Having a top-level righteousness, broad mind and strong will of pursuit thus standing on the higher realm are necessary to reach the very summit of excellence and achievement.

5.做一名兼具"中国情怀、世界视野"的当代 中国教育家

教育无国界，但教育家有祖国。我想，当代中国教育家的最大特征，应该是"中国情怀、世界视野"。只有兼具"中国情怀、世界视野"的教育家，才能有新作为、大作为，让人高看一眼，在中国教育史上占有一席之地；也只有兼具"中国情怀、世界视野"的当代中国教育家，才能在造福中国人民的同时，对世界教育事业和全人类文明进步作出自己的独特贡献。

5. Be an educationist in contemporary China with "Chinese feelings and global vision"

Education is a borderless cause, but the educationist has his Motherland. I think, the biggest characteristic of an educationist in contemporary China should be the one with "Chinese feelings and global vision". Only with both "Chinese feelings and global vision", shall this educationist have the aptitude to grasp the new and great accomplishments and to have people respect him. If this path is followed he may have a place in the history of Chinese education. Only with "Chinese feelings and global vision", shall we bring these benefits to Chinese people, and also make our unique contribution to global education and the civilization of all humankind.

6. 教育是一切

教育是诗篇；教育是哲学；教育是生命；教育是对话；教育是尊重；教育是科学；教育是艺术；教育是博爱。教育是一切。

6. Education is everything

Education is poetry; education is philosophy; education is life; education is conversation; education is respect; education is science; education is art; education is universal love. education is everything.

二、立德树人

II. Set High Moral Values and Cultivate People

7. 育人的本真是立德树人

　　教育的本真是育人，育人的本真是立德树人。教育是心灵与心灵的沟通，教育是灵魂与灵魂的碰撞；教育可以使人心灵净化，教育可以使人生命伟大。

7. The nature of nurturing people is to emphasize ethics

　　The nature of education is to nurture people, which has an emphasis on ethics. Education happens when one mind communicates with another, and when souls influence each other. Education can purify people's minds, and education can make lives great.

8. 立德树人是一项人心工程

　　立德树人是一项人心工程，最有效的途径是以心印心、以心塑心、以心传心。学校应该是精神高地，每一位教职员工都应该是传道者。我们将美好的心灵、高尚的品格传印给学生，学生毕业走向社会再传印给别人，如此传印下去，久久为功，和谐社会和美丽中国自会水到渠成。

8. The emphasis on ethics and the nurturing of people is a mind project

　　The emphasis on ethics and the nurturing of people is a project of the mind. The most effective path is to use heart to reflect, shape and communicate with another heart. Schools should be the uplands of the mind, and each member of the faculty and staff should be a preacher. We pass on the enquiring minds and noble personality to the students, and then they spread these gifts to others when they graduate and enter society. The spirit is passed on and on like this for a long time so it can work, creating a harmonious society. And a beautiful China will eventually fall into place.

9. 立德树人要将品德教育和能力教育结合起来

校园应该成为社会主义核心价值观建设的主阵地。我们今天讲立德树人，就是要用社会主义核心价值观这个"德"来培养学生、成就学生。立德，就是要让学生有一颗美丽而强大的中国心，这颗中国心里装着中国梦。树人，就是要让学生有报效祖国、服务社会、完美人生的能力。立德树人，实质上就是将品德教育和能力教育结合起来，培养品德高尚、能力高强的学生。

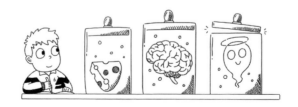

9. The emphasis on ethics and the nurturing of people requires education to combine moral character and capability

A campus should be the main ground for constructing core socialist values. Speaking of emphasizing ethics and nurturing people today, we should use core socialist values as the "moral value" to nurture students and to help them accomplish something. Emphasizing ethics means letting students have a beautiful and strong Chinese heart which contains the Chinese dream. Cultivating people means letting students have the capability to serve their Motherland and society, as well as developing a better life. The essence of emphasizing ethics and nurturing people is to combine education on both moral character and capability, and raising in students noble moral levels and strong abilities.

10. 德育是"根"的教育

德育是"根"的教育。学校的德育工作做得好，是国家和人民之福；学校的德育工作做得不好，是国家和人民之祸。学校德育工作应坚持五项原则：始终坚持把德育工作放在学校一切工作的首位；始终坚持把师德建设作为德育的基础；始终坚持把德育贯穿到学校生活的各个方面；始终坚持德育的时代性和针对性；始终坚持把道德教育和法治教育结合起来。

10. Moral education is on the "root"

Moral education is the "root" of a country. It is to the benefit of the country and its peoples' fortune if schools succeed in promoting moral education. It would be a disaster for the country and the people if schools fail in their work on moral education. There're five principles for schools to insist on in terms of moral education: we should insist on putting moral education above all other school work; we should insist that the construction of the teachers' morality is the base of moral education; we should insist on moral education penetrating into all aspects of school life; we should insist on timely and pertinent moral education, as well as carrying out moral and legal education as a whole.

11. 教育事业是灵魂事业

人活在世上，有三种生活：物质的生活、精神的生活、灵魂的生活。今天，我们培养人，一定不能局限于只教给学生谋生的技能，停留于物质的境界，一定不能局限于只教给学生欣赏文艺的法门，停留在精神的境界。我们培养人，一定要培养和提升学生的灵魂境界，让他们有美丽的心灵和高尚的灵魂。说到底，教育事业就是灵魂事业，教师是灵魂工程师。

11. The undertaking of education is about souls

There are 3 kinds of lives that a person can live: life with materials, life with spirit, and life with soul. Today, when we nurture people we should not limit their development to simply living skills and staying in the material state. Furthermore, we should not limit to leave them with the skills to admire arts so they would stay in the spirit realm. To cultivate people, we must foster and elevate students into the level where they shall have a beautiful mind and a noble soul. All in all, the undertaking of education is about souls, and teachers are the engineers of souls.

12. 培养受人尊敬的人

　　我们的教育，要从大处着眼，要从长远着眼，要从教学生如何成功转向教学生如何受人尊敬。与成功相比，受人尊敬是个大概念，是个高级概念，一个受人尊敬的人必然是个事业成功的人，但一个事业成功的人并不一定受人尊敬。我们的教育，就是要培养孩子既有过人的本领，更有强大的内心，内圣外王，臻于完人。教书育人，立德树人，就是要把立德、立功、立言统一起来，法古今完人，培养受人尊敬的人。

12. Nurture respectable people

We should extend our education into a bigger vision and a longer duration, which means teaching students to be respectable instead of just being successful. Compared with success, being respectable is a huge concept, and an advanced one. A respectable person must be someone with a successful career but one with successful career may not be respectable. Our education should raise children to not only have skillsets but also a strong heart. They should have a learning that is sound in both theory and in practice so they can be closer to perfection. Teaching and fostering students, together with the emphasis on ethics and the nurturing of people, means unifying the construction of morality, success and expression, with the learning from the saints in both history and current times, so as to raise respectable people.

13. 我们绝不培养精致的利己主义者

　　人大附中绝不培养精致的利己主义者，人大附中要培养有爱国情怀、英雄情怀、悲悯情怀的人。人大附中要培养有血性、有灵性、有理性、有诗性的人。人大附中要培养有本事、有担当的人。从人大附中走出来的人，要堂堂正正，浩浩荡荡。

13. We shall never raise sophisticated egoists

The High School Affiliated to Renmin University of China would never raise sophisticated egoists, instead, we would cultivate people with a spirit of patriotism, heroism and compassion. The High School Affiliated to Renmin University of China would raise people with a sense of courage, inspiration, rationality and poetry. The High School Affiliated to Renmin University of China would raise people who are capable and ready to take on responsibility. Graduates from The High School Affiliated to Renmin University of China should be dignified and imposing, but they should also be open and magnanimous.

人大附中早培班
"红色行动"公益
课程

三、爱与尊重

III. Love and Respect

14. 爱与尊重是教育工作者长久的诺言

爱是教育的最高境界，爱是自然流溢的奉献；尊重是教育的真谛，尊重是创造的源泉。

14. Love and respect is a long-term promise made by educators

Love is the highest state of education, and love is reflected through natural and spontaneous devotion. Respect is the essence of education, and respect breeds creativity.

15. 创造适合每位师生员工发展的教育

　　每个人都是鲜活而不可复制的生命个体，自由幸福地发展是他们的需要，创造一种让他们自由发展的教育是对生命的关爱和尊重。学校不仅应该成为每位学生幸福成长的乐园，也应该成为每位教职员工施展才华的沃土。我们要创造适合每位学生发展的教育，创造适合每位教职员工发展的教育。

15. Create an education that fits every teacher and student

　　Everyone is a lively and unique individual with a need to develop in a free and happy way. It shows love and respect to create an education system that allows them to develop freely. Schools should not only be a paradise for each student to grow up happily, but also be the fertile land for each faculty to display their talents. We should create an education structure that supports every student and faculty.

16. 我们要为儿童服务而不是为儿童做主

　　有学者说，人类文明的进化有三个重要阶段，第一个阶段是发现了人，将人从神的笼罩下解放出来；第二个阶段是发现了女性，将女性从男性的统治下解放出来；第三个阶段是发现了儿童，将儿童从对成人的依附中独立出来。当前，我们最应该做的事情，就是拨云见日，发现儿童。教育的出发点是学生，落脚点还是学生，社会、教师、家长都要为儿童服务，而不是为儿童做主。只有发现儿童，中国的基础教育才能进入新天地，迈向新时代。

16. We should serve children rather than make decisions for children

According to some scholars, there are 3 important stages in the evolution of human civilization. The first stage is the discovery of human nature, which released people out of the shadow of gods. The second stage is the discovery of the feminism, which freed women from the domination of men. The third stage is the discovery of children which gave them the independence from the dependence on the adult's world. At present what we should do most is to dispel the clouds to see the sun, which will help us to discover the children. The starting point of education is students, and the foothold of it is also children. Society, teachers and parents should all serve them rather than make decisions for them. Only by discovering children shall the basic education of China enter a new world, and step into a new era.

17. 人生因爱而幸福

　　教育，是我的人生大事；爱，是我在教育岗位上进德修业的"原动力"。我对学生付出了自己的爱，这种爱是无私的，不图回报的，而当你不图回报却得到了回报，当你爱孩子也被孩子们所爱的时候，这样的人生才是最幸福的。

17. Life is happy because of love

　　Education is the undertaking of my life, and love has been my "original motivation" to self study and to elevate moral standards as a teacher. I gave students my love, which is selfless without asking for anything in return. But when you receive something without expecting it, when the children you love actually love you back, that is the happiest moment in life.

四、中学教育之我见

IV. My Points of View on Secondary Education

18. 一流中学是一流大学的基础

　　教育事业是个整体，如果把教育比作金字塔的话，基础教育是塔基，大学教育是塔尖。一流大学不是空中楼阁，没有一流中学，难有一流大学。我们要从教育大国发展成为教育强国，必须建设一批世界一流的中学和大学。而我们创办世界一流学校的最高理念，是一切为了学生的全面而充分的发展。

18. A first class secondary school is the basis for a first class university

Education can have a life onto itself. If we compare education to a pyramid, then secondary education is the foundation, and university education is the spire. A first class university is not a castle in the air. Without a first class secondary school, there could be no first class university. If we want to become a country of strong education from a country with huge educational demand, we must build up a pool of top secondary schools and universities. The highest principle for us to build up the top schools of the world should be to provide the most comprehensive and thorough development of our students.

19. 中学是培养大成智慧的黄金时期

　　中学最适合通识教育，是培养大成智慧的黄金时期。在文科上有特长的学生具备良好的科学素养，在理科上有特长的学生具备良好的人文素养，这在中学是能够做到的。错过了中学时代，一旦进了大学，文理学科泾渭分明，壁垒森严，要搞通识教育，难度不知要增加多少倍。因此，我们搞中学教学改革，讲提升中学办学质量，主攻方向就应该放在开展通识教育、培养大成智慧上。

19. The secondary school period is the Golden Age for cultivating meta-synthetic wisdom

Secondary school is most suitable for carrying out general education, and it's the Golden Era for cultivating meta-synthetic wisdom. Secondary school can provide students who are specialized in liberal arts with excellent science accomplishments, and those who specialize in science subjects with outstanding grasp of the humanities. If the importance of middle school phase is neglected, the difficulty to carry out general education would be many times more once one enters university, because there the science subjects and liberal arts are quite distinct from each other, and the barrier between them is strongly fortified. Thus, when we reform secondary education and speak of improving educational quality of secondary schools, the main direction is to develop general education and cultivate meta-synthetic wisdom.

20. 中学教育必须是独立完整的体系

　　我一直认为，中学教育必须是独立完整的体系，必须有自己独立完整的目标。但今天，中学只是小学、中学、大学这一教育链条中的一个环节，中学的任务好像就是给大学输送生源。这样的定位，对中学教育的伤害是致命的。中学教育不独立、不完整，就形不成大格局，做不了大文章，也不可能有大作为、大成就。

20. Secondary education must be an independent and complete system

I always believe that secondary education must be an independent and complete system, and must have their own independent and complete objectives. But nowadays, secondary schools seem to become only one link in the educational chain which contains elementary and secondary schools and college. The mission of secondary schools seems to only supply students to universities. Such positioning can do lethal damage to the education of secondary schools. If secondary education is not independent and complete, there shall not be a big picture, nor can secondary education receive noticeable accomplishments and achievements.

21. 中学教育要为学生的发展 "壮腰健肌"

如果把人才成长的过程比作一个人的肌体，那么中学阶段就是这个人的腰，腰部无力，人是站立不起来的。因此，基础教育首先要为学生打好宽厚坚实的基础，为他们未来的发展 "壮腰健肌"。

21. Secondary education should "strengthen the waistline and exercise muscles" for the development of the students

If we compare the growth of a talent to a person's body, then the period of secondary education is the person's waistline. With a powerless waist, one cannot stand up. Therefore, basic education shall first of all build a solid foundation for the students, and shall "strengthen the waistline and exercise muscles" for their future development.

22. 中学教育要"以德为先"

　　中学时代是人一生最重要的时期，是完成身心发育，奠定情感基础，形成世界观的关键时期。这是一段蛹虫蜕变为蝴蝶、丑小鸭长成白天鹅的精彩时光。中学教育担负着培养学生内在道德观形成的重任，必须"以德为先"，校长、教师要以心育心、以德养德，在言传身教中将人性的光芒撒向青少年的内心世界中。

人大附中掠影

22. Education in secondary schools should "have morality taking precedence"

The phase of secondary school is one of the most important in a person's life. It is the critical phase where they complete their physical and mental growth, as well as setting up their emotional foundation and forming a world outlook. This is a splendid time where the caterpillar turns into a butterfly, and the ugly duckling grows into a white swan. Secondary education takes on the responsibilities to help children form inner moral values so it must "have morality taking precedence". The headmasters and teachers should use their hearts to educate the students' hearts, and use morality to raise morality, to shine the light of humanity into the internal world of the young people from the educator's own precepts and examples.

五、炼就好校长之名与实

V. Trained Well for the Reputation and Practice of a Good Principal

23. 做一个优秀的"领跑人"

　　我对"校长"含义的理解，最深切之处就在于，校长是个"领跑人"——面向世界、面向未来，领着全校的教职员工不停地奔跑，领着一茬又一茬的孩子不停地奔跑。从做校长的那一天起，我就一直用"领跑人"自喻，始终以做优秀的"领跑人"自勉。做一个"领跑人"，首先自己得跑；做一个优秀的"领跑人"，必须跑得比别人快，跑得比别人远，需要过人的综合素质，需要过人的精神状态，需要比别人思想更超前，更勇于创新，善于创新。

23. Be an excellent "front runner"

My understanding of the meaning of "principal", is that of a "front runner"— who faces the world, looks to the future, leads the faculty and staff to run without stopping, and leads group after group of children in their continuous development. Since the first day I became a principal I have always been comparing myself to a "front runner", and encouraging myself to be an excellent "front runner". Being a "front runner", first of all, means to run for oneself, and being an excellent "front runner" means you must run faster and further than others. It requires exceptional overall quality, and requires exceptional spiritual status. It requires one to think ahead of all others, have more courage to innovate and be better at innovation.

24. 好校长要真人办真事

　　教育是个大课题，它与个人、家庭，与时代、社会密切相关；教育又是一项伟大的事业，重要到如陶行知先生所言："在教师手里操着幼年人的命运，便是操着民族和人类的命运。"名校长要做到名副其实，就要真懂教育，真想为教育奉献，真关心教育的发展，就要说真话、办实事，解决实际问题。一句话：要真人办真事。

24. A good principal should be an authentic person who is doing practical things

Education is a big topic and it relates closely to individuals, families and to the time and the society. Education is also a great undertaking, and its importance is expressed in what Tao Xingzhi said, "In their hands, teachers hold the life of youngsters, which actually means they hold the fate of the nation and all human kind." A principal of a well-known secondary school should live up to his name. This means to really understand education, be devoted to education, and be genuinely concerned about the development of education. It also means to speak the truth, do practical things and solve actual problems. In a word, be an authentic person who is doing practical things.

25. 干正确的事比正确地干事更重要

　　写文章有写什么和怎么写的问题，当校长管理学校，也有个做什么和怎么做的问题。一个校长要"想干事，能干事，会干事"，还要"干好事，不惹事"。我的最大体会就是，做什么比怎么做更重要，干正确的事比正确地干事更重要。干正确的事是大前提，大前提成立了，一顺百顺。

25. Doing the right thing is more important than doing things in a right way

　　If we write an article, there is the problem of what to write and how to express it. When running a school as a principal, there is the problem of what to do and how to do it. A principal should "be willing to do his job, and be capable of doing it", and he should also "do good things without causing trouble". My biggest experience is, what you are doing is more important than how to do it, and doing the right thing is more important than doing things in a right way. Doing the right thing is the precondition. Once the precondition is set, everything will go smoothly.

26. 学校管理要理顺关系

　　管理，管理，既要管更要理。从某种意义上讲，搞管理也要理顺关系。把各种关系理顺了，管理工作自然也就顺了。如何理顺关系？可以概括为四句话："对上多争取，对外多联系，对下多支持，中间多默契。""对上多争取"，就是多争取上级领导部门的扶持；"对外多联系"，就是广泛联系社会力量支持学校工作；"对下多支持"，就是保护好、发挥好全体教职员工的积极性和创造性，全力支持部下的工作；"中间多默契"，就是领导班子之间要团结，各部门之间要协作。

26. School management is about managing good working relationships

Management means not only to manage but also to administrate. In some ways, good management means managing good relationships with others. Once all kinds of working relationships are straightened out, the management work will be much smoother. How do we straighten out these relationships? It can be summarized into 4 sentences: "Strive for more support from the superiors. Make more contact with external parties. Offer more support to the subordinates. Share more understanding with peers." "Strive for more support from the superiors" means to get more support from the superior departments. "Make more contact with external parties" means to widely contact social forces to support school work. "Offer more support to the subordinates" means to protect and elaborate the positivity and innovation of all faculty and staff, and to fully support the work of subordinates. "Share more understanding with peers" means the administrators should unite together, and different departments should cooperate with each other.

27. 浪费人才是校长的品质问题

　　一个学校绝对不能藏龙卧虎，是龙就得让它腾，是虎就得让它跃，龙藏着虎卧着，就是一种最大的浪费。对校长来说，发现不了人才是水平问题，而浪费人才就是品质问题。校长要把方方面面优秀人才的积极性、创造性调动好、保护好、发挥好。用崇高的理想激励人才，用宏大的事业凝聚人才，用合理的待遇奖励人才，用深厚的感情留住人才。

27. It would be a principal's character problem to waste talent

A school should never have crouching tigers and hidden dragons. If it's a dragon then it should be set flying, and if it's a tiger it should be set jumping. Making a dragon hidden or a tiger crouch would be a huge waste. For a principal, it's a capability problem if he cannot discover talent, whereas it would be a character problem to waste talent. A principal should stimulate, protect and develop the positivity and creativity of talents in all aspects. Noble ideals should be used to inspire talented people, grand causes should be used to gather talents, reasonable welfare and benefit should be rewarded to talents, and gratitude should be expressed in order to keep talents.

28. 校长要同时扮演好制约者和激励者两个角色

　　制约与激励是管理大厦的两根支柱，这两根支柱不能一根长一根短，也不能一根粗一根细，否则大厦就要出问题。制约机制是告诉大家不能做什么，激励机制是提倡大家应该做什么。制约机制要"密不透风"，即规章制度要周全；激励机制要"疏可走马"，即给大家发挥主观能动性和创造性提供广阔的空间。校长要同时扮演好两个角色：在执行制约机制时，要"金刚怒目"，敢于"管"；在执行激励机制时，则要"菩萨慈眉"，善于"奖"。一个管不住教职工的校长不是好校长，一个不能让教职工充分发挥创造才能的校长也不是好校长。

28. A principal should play the roles of both inhibitor and stimulator

Restriction and stimulation are the two pillars of the management mansion. These two pillars can't be one long and the other short, or one thick and the other thin. In that way there would be problems with the construction. Restriction mechanism is to tell people what shouldn't be done, and stimulation mechanism is to encourage people in what they should do. The method of restriction should be "airtight", which means all rules and regulations should be complete and thorough. The method of stimulation should be "widely open", which means to provide an open space for people to take the initiative and achieve creativity. A principal should play both roles in a right way. When implementing restriction, the headmaster should "glare like a temple door god with anger", which means to dare to "supervise". While implementing the stimulation, a headmaster should be "kind as a Buddha", who is good at "rewarding". A headmaster who cannot manage his faculty and staff well is not a good one, and one cannot be a good headmaster if he does not have faculties and staff fully develop their creativity.

29. 好校长要能激活每一个细胞

如果将学校比作一个乐团，校长就是乐团的指挥，教职工就是拉大提琴、小提琴、吹长号、打架子鼓的乐手。只有激活每一个细胞，才能形成智慧的合力与力量的合力；只有激活每一个细胞，才能带动学校飞速发展。校长应该是一位运筹帷幄的棋手，把每一个棋子都放在适当的位置，既要让每一个岗位都有最适合的人，也要让每个人都做适合自己的事，还要让每个上岗的人都有责任意识和忧患意识。

29. A good principal should be able to activate every cell

If we compare a school to an orchestra, the principal is the conductor, and faculty and staff are the cellists, violinists, trombonists and drummers. Only by activating every single one of the cells, shall we form the joint forces of wisdom and power; only by activating every single one of the cells shall we drive the school to a better and swifter development. A principal should be a chess player who controls the situation well in advance, and can put every chess piece into the most suitable place. This means that every post should have the most adequate person, and everyone does things that they are most capable of. Also, each person in position should have a sense of responsibility and a good work ethic.

30. 当好一把手要"谋事在众，决断在己，成事在众"

　　如何当好一把手？可以用三句话概括，即"谋事在众，决断在己，成事在众"。所谓"谋事在众"是指决策之前，一定要充分发挥民主，广泛征求大家的意见，集中大家的智慧；"决断在己"是指在充分发扬民主，广泛征求大家意见的基础上，作为一把手的校长要勇于拍板，敢于担当；"成事在众"则是指一旦决策之后，不必事必躬亲，要放手让大家去干，靠大家的共同努力去把事情做成。

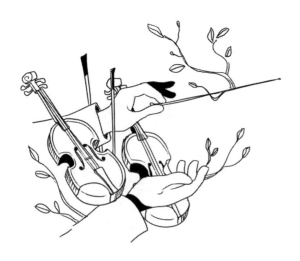

30. The first in command should "consult with the public, make decisions by oneself, and achieve together with the public"

How to be the first in command? It can be summarized into 3 sentences: "Consult with the public, make decisions by oneself, and accomplish depending on the public". "Consult with the public" refers to fully implementing democracy, widely listening to the public ideas and collecting public intelligence before making decisions. "Make decisions by oneself" means as the first in command, a principal should be brave enough to make decisions and dare to take responsibility on the basis of full implementation of democracy and widely collection of public ideas. "Achieve together with the public" refers to once the decision is made, it is not necessary to take every little thing in hand, but to adequately release work to everyone and make things happen by joint efforts of the whole team.

31. 好校长必须具有人格魅力

　　当好校长必须具有人格魅力。一是"无欲则刚"。无私欲，无邪念，一身正气，两袖清风，责在人先，利在人后，才能立世有威信，改革有底气。二是"有容乃大"。器量须大，心胸须宽，要记人之功，容人之过。三是带着爱心工作。要爱群、乐群、利群。四是带着激情工作。要有干事的冲动，成功的渴望，不断提出新的奋斗目标。

31. A good principal should have personal charm

A good principalr should have personal charm. Firstly is to "be austere and have no selfish desires". A principal should be like this: no selfish desires, no wicked ideas, surrounded by healthy atmosphere, remain honorable, step forward when it's time to take responsibilities, stay behind when benefits come. Only with these actions shall one establish credibility, and then have the basis and self-confidence to bring about reform. Secondly is that "tolerance brings respect". One should be broad-minded and open-minded, should remember others' contribution, and tolerate others' faults. Thirdly, one should work with a loving heart, should love the crowd, be happy in the crowd and do good for the crowd. Fourthly, one should work with passion. One should have the passion to do something, the desire for success, and always seek new objectives to fight for.

32. 做教育家型校长的十二条心语

中国需要一大批教育家型的校长。我总结出做教育家型校长的十二条心语。

一是事业心。是一位热爱教育事业，具有高尚品德，能将自己的一生奉献给教育事业的人。

二是理想目标。是一位有思想、有实践、有理念、有理想、有高远目标的人。

三是赤子之心。是一位有中国心、中国情、中国梦，"苟利国家生死以，岂因祸福避趋之"的人。

四是奋斗精神。是一位为了实现远大理想，坚韧不拔，执着追求，奋斗不息的人；是一位具有不断探索，不断实验，敢于冒险，永不言败，永不气馁，勇于承担责任的习惯和品质的人。

五是爱与尊重。是能够将爱与尊重的理念深入骨髓和血液，自然流溢在行动中的人。

六是解放学生。是一位能够解放学生，解放教师，解放员工，全心全意为他们服务，而不是替他们做决定的人。

七是培养受人尊敬的人。努力培养学生学会尊敬他人，成为受人尊敬的人，绝不培养精致的利己主义者，要培养堂堂正正的中国人。

八是勤学习，善思考，细分析，勇创新。为了实现理想目标，不断学习，不断思考，跟上时代的脚步，熔铸中外教育精华，坚持综合创新，探索未来教育的人。

九是博大胸怀。能够吃大苦，耐大劳，面对有问题的人，能够容他、忍他、让他，再过一段时间再看他、再教育他，在艰难困苦面前不退缩，在被冤枉陷害情况下仍向前的人。

十是研究。要深刻了解学生的成长规律，要认真研究学生的心理发展特点，能科学地按教育规律办教育的人。

十一是永不满足。未来教育家型校长应低调做人，谦虚谨慎，永不满足，永远前行，不断学习，不断进步，成就事业，成就理想，艰苦奋斗，坚决实现自己梦想的人。

十二是实践。教育家不是吹出来的，应该是干出来的。看教育家的教育思想、教育理念、教育实践怎么样，应该到他的学校去看看，看他的教育思想是否深入人心，是否是真正受人拥护的人。

32. 12 quotes of reflections on being a principal of an educationist style

China needs many principals who are of a true educationist style. I have summarized 12 quotes of reflections on being a principal of educationist style.

First is the sense of responsibility. One should be a person who loves the education undertaking, possesses noble morality and can devote one's whole life to the cause of education.

The second is the ideal objective. One should be a person who has thought, practice, theory, ideal and a long-sighted objective.

The third is man's natural kindness. One should have a Chinese heart, Chinese emotion and Chinese dream, and be a person who believes in "the conviction that I will do whatever it takes to serve my country even at the cost of my own life, regardless of fortune or misfortune to myself."

The fourth is the striving spirit. One should be a person who's persistent and dauntless, with a spirit of pursuit, and strives without hesitation in order to realize the grand ideal. One should have the habit and quality of continuous exploration, persistent experiment, daring to challenge, never giving up and the courage to take responsibility.

The fifth is love and respect. One should infiltrate the concept of love and respect into the bones and blood, and this will be naturally evident in our actions.

The sixth is to liberate students. One should be able to liberate students, liberate teachers, liberate employees and serve them whole-heartedly instead of making decisions for them.

The seventh is to cultivate respectable people. One should strive to nurture students to respect others and become respectable individuals. One should never raise egoists but to cultivate dignified and outstanding Chinese people.

The eighth is to diligently learn, be good at thinking, always analyze with care, and dare to innovate. In order to achieve the ideal goal, one should keep studying and reflecting, consider current trends, blend the best educational practices of both China and abroad, insist on comprehensive innovation, and look to the future of education.

The ninth is to have a broad mind. One should be capable of bearing huge hardship and enduring hard work. One should firstly tolerate, endure and yield to the people with problems, then check and educate them after a while. One shall not step back against difficulties and hardships, and should keep heading forward even when he was treated unjustly and framed.

The tenth is to investigate. One should deeply learn about the growing pattern of the students, should carefully investigate the developing characteristics of the psychology of students, and should scientifically practice education following the correct pattern of education.

The eleventh is never to be satisfied. A principal of future educationist style should be the one who keeps a low profile, is modest and prudent, never satisfied, keeps heading forward, continuously studies, keeps making progress, achieving his undertaking, realizing ideals, being hard-working and is determined to realize his dreams.

The twelfth is to practice. One doesn't make an educationist only by bragging about it, but by actual work. In order to see the educational ideas, concepts and practice of an educationist, we should go to his school and see if his educational ideas are widely accepted, and whether he is someone who is truly supported by people.

六、教育改革与创新

VI. Educational Reform and Innovation

33. 创新理念

　　突破能创新，变通能创新，融合能创新，反思能创新；压力能创新，理想能创新，目标能创新，需求能创新；激励能创新，实践能创新，执着能创新，追求能创新；卓越能创新，完美能创新，求真能创新，务实能创新；时时能创新，处处能创新，事事能创新，人人能创新。

33. Concepts on innovation

　　Breakthrough can be innovated; flexibility can be innovated; integration can be innovated; introspection can be innovated; pressure can be innovated; ideal can be innovated; objective can be innovated; needs can be innovated; stimulation can be innovated; practice can be innovated; persistence can be innovated; pursuit can be innovated; excellence can be innovated; perfection can be innovated; truth-seeking can be innovated; pragmatism can be innovated; every moment can have innovation; everywhere can have innovation; everything can be innovated; everyone can have innovation.

34. 创新过程理念

　　不断地思考与寻找，不断地寻找与变通，在变通中寻求突破，在突破中形成决策。

34. Concept on the innovation process

Keep thinking and seeking, keep seeking and adapting; pursue breakthrough through adaptations, and form decisions in this breakthrough.

35. 常规与创新是处于动态之中

　　没有常规就没有稳定，没有稳定就难以创新；而没有创新则失去了发展的动力，教育的生命将走向枯竭。常规与创新并非一成不变，而是处于动态之中。今日之常规，可能是昨日创新之成果；今日之创新，可能成为明日之常规。当教育创新走向成熟之时，往往就成为新的教育常规。

35. Routine and innovation are always in motion

There shall be no stability without routine, and without stability it would be difficult to innovate, and we will lose the motivation of development without innovation, and the life of education will come to the end. Routine and innovation are not unalterable, but in motion. Today's routine might be the result of yesterday's innovation; today's innovation could be tomorrow's routine. When educational innovation becomes mature, it usually will become a new routine of education.

创新人才教育
研究会简介

36. 教育创新要慎提"不怕失败，宽容失败"

　　创新总会伴随风险和失败，但教育创新则要慎提"不怕失败，宽容失败"。一项科学实验可以有 666 次失败，但中学教学创新、教育创新的一次失败就可能贻误一个班级、一个年级甚至几个年级的学生，这样的失败成本太高，损失太大，谁也没有资格冒这样的风险。因此，我们一方面要大力提倡教育创新，另一方面又要提醒中学校长和教师：创新之前一定要做好充分的调查研究，深思熟虑，谋定而动，并且争取一动而成；一定要将创新的风险和成本降到最低。

36. Educational innovation should be cautious on mentioning "not afraid of failure, tolerating failure"

Innovation always comes with risk and failure, but educational innovation should be cautious on mentioning "not afraid of failure, tolerating failure". One scientific experiment can fail for 666 times, but the failure of innovation on secondary education could mislead one class, one or even several grades. The failing cost would be too high and the loss would be so big that nobody would be willing to accept. Therefore, on one hand we should strongly encourage educational innovation; on the other hand we should remind the principals and teachers in secondary schools that a full investigation and research should be carried out before innovation. Think thoroughly, move after properly strategizing, and strive for success at the first strike; we must reduce the risk and cost to the lowest scale.

37. 素质教育改革要"截断众流、随波逐流"

　　我用"截断众流、随波逐流"这八个字来概括对素质教育的认识。所谓"截断众流",就是要在第一时间中止每个人不好的意念、不好的习惯、不好的方法,而教给他良好的意念、良好的习惯、良好的方法。所谓"随波逐流",就是及时发现每个人的潜能和特长,尊重他的个性,挖掘他的潜能,发挥他的特长,给他最适合的教育。对教育工作者来说,"截断众流",是有所作为;"随波逐流",在一定意义上是无为而治。"截断众流",是侧重以教师为本;"随波逐流",是侧重以学生为本。合起来,就是教育工作完整意义上的以人为本,就是教学过程中完整的教学相长。

37. The reform on the education for all-round development requires to "dam the flow, go with the wave"

I would use 7 words as "dam the flow, go with the wave" to summarize my view on the education for all-round development. "Dam the flow" means to stop one's bad concept, habit and method at the moment when we see one, and teach him the correct concept, habit and method. "Go with the wave" is to discover each one's potential and specialty, respect his characteristic, dig out his potential, develop his specialty and gives him the most suitable education. For an educator, "dam the flow" means to do something; "go with the wave" in some ways means to govern by doing nothing that goes against nature. "Dam the flow" is to emphasize on the teachers' side; "go with the wave" is to focus on being student-oriented. Combining these two is the whole meaning of being people-oriented in the work of education, as well as a complete teaching and learning, mutually-beneficial process in education.

38. 教育改革的核心是课程改革

　　课程在学校教育教学中处于核心地位，教育的目标价值主要通过课程来体现和实施。因此，课程改革是教育教学改革的核心内容。没有课程改革，教育改革必然会成为空中楼阁。课程改革的目标，应该是创设适合每个学生发展的教育，让每个学生都能感受到学习的乐趣，为终身学习和终身发展奠定基础。

38. The core of education reform is curriculum reform

　　Curriculum lies in the core position of education and teaching in schools, and the target value of education is mainly reflected and implemented through curriculum. So, the core of education reform is curriculum reform. Without curriculum reform, education reform will just be a castle in the air. The objective of curriculum reform should be to design and establish an education that suits the development of each student, making all of them enjoy the pleasure of study, and lay a foundation for a life-long learning and life-long development.

39. 课程改革要处理好变与不变的关系

　　课程改革要正确处理好变与不变的关系。在中国的传统哲学中，"化"是最高境界，"化"中有变也有不变，是变与不变的有机结合。从某种意义上讲，课程改革也是一种不断的进化，首先要弄清楚哪些东西必须改，哪些东西不能改，进而正确处理好变与不变的关系，做到"变"中有"常"，进入"化"的境界。一个成熟的改革家应该客观地对待过去、准确地把握现实、科学地预测未来，在变与不变、继承和改革中显示智慧。过去受应试教育的制约，我们的课程设置确实有许多弊端，非改不可，但我们在改革时不能把"洗澡水"和"婴儿"一起倒掉了。"婴儿"是中国的中学课程设置特别重视基础知识。在中国读书的中学毕业生基础知识扎实，全世界公认。这个好传统一定要坚持。

39. The relation between the changed and the unchanged should be handled well in curriculum reform

The relation between the changed and the unchanged should be handled well in curriculum reform. According to traditional Chinese philosophy, "transformation" is the highest state, which contains the changed and the unchanged. And it's the organic combination of the two. In a way, curriculum reform is a continuous evolution. First we should figure out what needs to be changed, and what needs to stay the same, and then we can handle the relation between the changed and the unchanged correctly to achieve a status where "routine" lies in "change" to enter the realm of "transformation". A mature reformer should objectively treat the past, accurately grasp the present, scientifically predict the future, and demonstrate wisdom in the changed and the unchanged, the succession and the reform. In the past, there are many disadvantages in our curriculum setting due to the constraint of exam-oriented education, and they must be changed. But we shouldn't throw away the "baby" along with the "bath water". "Baby" here refers to the fact that the curriculum setting of secondary education in our country attaches great importance to basic knowledge. It is acknowledged by the whole world that graduates from Chinese secondary schools are with solid foundation in basic knowledge. We must stick to this good tradition.

40. 课程改革要处理好增加与减少的关系

课程改革要正确处理好增加和减少的关系。应该说课程改革面临着一对矛盾，一方面是知识量、信息量只能增加不能减少，另一方面是要通过课程改革真正减轻学生负担，让孩子们学习、生活得快乐。要解决好这对矛盾，唯一的途径就是提高教学质量，从某种意义上说，就是现在的一堂课要产生过去两堂课甚至几堂课的效益；要让学生既学得多、学得好，又学得不累。

40. The relation of increasing and reducing should be handled well in curriculum reform

The interconnection between increasing and reducing should be handled well in curriculum reform. Actually the curriculum reform faces a paradox: on one hand, the knowledge and information quantity should only be increased rather than be reduced, while on the other hand, the students' burden needs to be reduced for real through curriculum reform to make them happy in learning and living. In order to solve this paradox, the only way is to improve the quality of teaching. In some ways, it means one class of today should have the same outcome of 2 or even several classes in the past; students should learn more and learn well, without being worn out at the same time.

41. 课程改革要处理好有意义和有意思的关系

　　课程改革要正确处理好有意义和有意思的关系。长期以来，我们改革的兴奋点和注意力更多地集中在有意义上，这更多的是站在教育者的立场看问题、想问题。站在学生的立场看问题、想问题，则应该更关注是否有意思，学生更愿意在有意思中接受有意义。这就像吃饭，家长强调的是有营养，孩子重视的是有滋味，他们更乐于在美味中接受营养。我们进行课程改革的着眼点和着力点，应该在"既有意义，也有意思"上，给学生提供的"营养套餐"，一定要让学生"吃"得有滋有味。

41. The relation of being meaningful and being interesting should be handled well in curriculum reform

The interconnection between being meaningful and being interesting should be handled well in curriculum reform. For a long time, we have been putting the stimulating point and attention on whether it's meaningful, and this is more of seeing and thinking the issue from the perspective of an educator. If seeing and thinking from the students' point of view, we should focus more on whether it's interesting, because students are more willing to accept meaning from amusement. Just like eating, parents emphasize nutrition but the children are more interested in the taste, and they are more willing to absorb nutrition from delicacy. The starting point and application point of our curriculum reform should focus on "not only meaningful, but also interesting" so that we provide students with nutritive set meal, and make sure they eat it with enjoyment.

42. 改革创新课堂教学首要的是培养孩子的自学能力

　　改革创新课堂教学是提高教学质量、培养学生创新精神和创新能力的重要途径，我觉得摆在第一位的是培养孩子的自学能力。自学，既是自己学习，更是自主学习。自己学习好理解，自主学习，是指在自己学习中有独立的思考。相比之下，自主学习，是更重要的自学。人的一生，即使读完博士，最长的在校跟着老师学习时间也就二十多年。目前，人的平均寿命是七十三岁，由此可见，人的学习，绝大部分时间是自学。有人预测，在中等发达国家，人人都接受过或多或少的学校教育，传统意义上的文盲已经消亡了。以后，文盲这个词，也许指的是那些离开学校后不能通过自学来更新知识的人。进一步讲，即使是在学校学习期间，我们自学的东西也肯定比从老师、从课堂上学到的东西多。再进一步讲，即使是听老师讲，也要加入自己的思考。因此，自学才是学习的常态，才是学习的核心。

42. The priority of reforming and innovating classroom teaching is to cultivate the self-learning ability of children

Reforming and innovating the classroom teaching is a very important way to improve teaching quality, as well as cultivating students to have a spirit and capability of innovation. I think raising children with self-learning ability comes first. Self-learning ability, not only refers to study by oneself, but also means to actively study. Active self-learning means to have independent thinking during the self-studying process. Compared with others, active self-studying is a much more critical self-learning. In one's whole life, the longest study time with teachers would be only more than 20 years, even to those who finish a doctor degree. At present the average life-span of a human being is 73 years old. This means that people are mostly learning by oneself in the majority of their time. It is estimated that people are more or less educated in moderately developed countries, so there are no more illiterate people according to traditional concepts. In the future, the words "illiterate person" maybe refers to those who can't update their knowledge system by self-learning after leaving school. Furthermore, even when we are still in school, the knowledge we can get by self-learning would be definitely more than what we receive from teachers and lessons. Besides, even when we listen to our teachers, we should add in our own thinking. As a result, self-learning is the routine of study, and the core of study.

七、教师队伍建设

VII. Development of the Faculty Team

43. 教师队伍建设是学校最基本的建设

　　学校工作好比是大树，干部队伍、员工队伍、教师队伍好比是枝干、树叶、花朵和果实。一般说来，直接开花结果的只有教师队伍。因此，教师队伍建设是学校最基本的建设。

43. The Development of faculty teams is the most basic construction of a school

School work is like a huge tree, and the teams of administrators, faculty and staff are branches, leaves, flowers and fruits. Generally speaking, only the team of faculty can blossom and yield fruits directly. Thus, the development of faculty team is the most basic construction of a school.

44. 让教师成才是学校最根本的工作

如果说"学生成才是教育工作的着眼点"的话，那么，"教师成才是教育工作的着力点"。教师是教育事业的根本，教师是教育事业的元气，我们为教育事业培本固元，最根本的工作就是让教师成才。

44. It's a school's most essential work to have teachers succeed in their career

If we say "making students become useful people is the starting point of educational work", then "having teachers succeed in their career is the application point of educational work". Teachers are the foundation and the vitality of the cause of education. If we want to keep the foundation and vitality in a solid way for the cause of education, the most essential work is to have teachers succeed in their career.

45. 职业、敬业、乐业是教师成才的"三部曲"

　　教师怎样才能成才？我总结了"六字真言"——职业、敬业、乐业。职业，就是要符合从事教师工作的所有硬件要求，我们必须不断严格教师的资格认证，不断抬高教师的职业门槛；敬业，就是要崇敬教育工作；乐业，就是要热爱教育工作，在教书育人中享受快乐，在与学生一起成长中体味幸福。只有热爱，才能在工作中有热情，有激情，有创造力；才能出类拔萃，成为人才。职业、敬业、乐业，是教师成才的"三部曲"。

人大附中联合
学校总校简介
（2019 年）

45. The "trilogy" of making teachers succeed in their career is being professional, dedicated and enthusiastic

How to make a teacher succeed in his career? I summarized "3 mantras"── being professional, dedicated and enthusiastic. Being professional, is to fit in all qualifications required of being a teacher. We must keep the qualification standards of teachers in a strict way, and keep elevating the professional level for one to be qualified to be a teacher. Being dedicated, a respect for education; being enthusiastic, a love of education, the enjoyment of the process of teaching and cultivating people, and the experience of happiness in the progress of growing with the students. Only with love, shall one have enthusiasm and passion; shall one become outstanding and be a talent. Being professional, dedication and professional enthusiasm, are the "trilogy" of making teachers succeed in their career.

46. 为中学教师成才支招

　　中学和大学特别是科研型大学不同，中学教师的成才绝大多数是岗位成才，具有很强的实践性。因此，中学培养教师成才，主要途径就是搭台子，压担子，把教师特别是青年教师放到重要岗位上去锻炼。再有就是激励和赏识。好孩子是夸出来的，好妻子是夸出来的，好丈夫是夸出来的，好教师也是夸出来的。对取得成绩的教师，对有进步的教师，学校一定要多激赏，一定要多表扬，包括精神上荣誉上的激赏，也包括物质上待遇上的激赏。

46. My advice on making teachers of secondary schools succeed in their career

Secondary schools are different from universities and special research universities. Most teachers of secondary school are usually successful during their duty, which is generally very practical. Therefore, if a secondary school wants to make its teachers succeed in their career, the main approach is to establish a platform and give them responsibilities to let the teachers especially young ones to be trained for important posts. Secondly, schools should show them encouragement and appreciation. Excellent children, wives and husbands are all made by giving them compliments, so are outstanding teachers. The school must encourage and praise the teachers more often who have made achievements or progress, and this encouragement includes words of appreciation, as well as physical and remunerative rewards.

47. 学校打造高水平教师队伍的五个要点

学校打造高水平的教师队伍要注重以下五个方面：一是点燃激情，让教师树立为教育事业献身的精神；二是搭建平台，让教师实现人生的价值；三是重视团队建设，建立有利于教师共同发展的机制；四是加强校本培训，引领、促进教师成才；五是关心教师身心健康，营造宽松和谐的工作氛围。

47. Five pillars on developing a high-level faculty team for a school

A school should pay attention to the following 5 aspects when it tries to develop a high-level faculty team: the first one is to light up the passion, and encourage teachers to establish the spirit to dedicate themselves into the education undertaking. The second one is to establish a platform for teachers to realize their value of life. The third one is to attach importance to team building, and to form a mechanism that is in favor of teachers' common development. The fourth one is to reinforce school-based trainings to lead and facilitate teachers to succeed. The fifth is to care about the physical and mental health of the teachers, and provide them with a comfortable and harmonious working atmosphere.

48.教师首先是人格之师

教育的核心不是传授知识，而是让学生学会做人。"师者"，首先是"传道"，以自己道德问题的正确标尺去引导学生。立德树人首先要立师德，有师德，然后才有生德。一个教师首先应该成为人格之师、道德之师，要善于用自己的言语、行为、情趣、品格去影响学生；其次，才是知识之师。

48. A teacher should first teach personality

The core of education is not to pass knowledge, but to have the students learn how to be a person. "Being a teacher" first requires to "teach principles", and to use his own right standard scale on morality to guide students. In order to set high moral values and cultivate people, we should first set high moral values for teachers. When those are established, the moral values of students will in turn be generated. A teacher should first be the teacher of personality and morality, and should be good at using his words, behaviors, temperament and characteristics to affect students; then, he shall be the teacher of knowledge.

49. 今天的教师必须是一个"阳光教师"

今天的教师必须是一个"阳光教师"。其一，"坦荡荡"而不"常戚戚"，不会沉湎于"小我"而不能自拔，患得患失；其二，积极乐观，总相信努力能改变一切，总相信明天比今天好，不会为一时一事的挫折而消沉悲观；其三，有感恩之心和热爱之情，对生活、对工作、对家庭、对学生充满感恩和热爱之情。一个心理不阳光，情商有缺陷的教师，不是我们所要求的成才教师。

49. Teachers of today must be a "dynamic teacher"

Teachers of today must be a "dynamic teacher". Firstly, a teacher should "be open and poised" instead of "unhappy and worried", and will not be indulged in "one's ego", unable to get out, nor only worry about his own personal gains and losses. Secondly, a teacher should be positive and optimistic, and always believe that efforts can change everything and that tomorrow is better than today; they shouldn't be depressed and pessimistic due to a single matter every now and then. Thirdly, a teacher should have a grateful heart and enthusiasm. He should be fully grateful and enthusiastic for life, for work, for family and for students. A teacher who's mentally gloomy and has a defect in EQ is not the one we want to succeed in a teaching career.

八、汲取中外精华，创办未来教育

VIII. Extract Domestic and Foreign Essence, Found an Education of the Future

50. 中西方教育应该相互取长补短

中西方的教育各有长短。中国的传统教育长于传授，具有基础知识扎实而动手能力弱的特点；西方的教育长于体验，具有动手能力强而基础知识不够扎实的特点。中西方教育应该相互取长补短。我们应该一手抓继承性常规教学，一手抓教育教学创新，两手都不能放松。

50. Chinese and western educations should learn from each other's strengths and close the gap

Chinese and western educations have their own advantages and disadvantages. Traditional Chinese education is strong at lecturing, and its characteristics are solid basic knowledge but weak practical skills; western education is good at experience and its characteristics are strong practical skills with a rather unsteady basic knowledge. Chinese and western educations should learn from each other's strengths and close the gap. We should on one hand, inherit the excellent regular teaching, while on the other hand, focus on educational innovation, and shall not loosen any of these two.

51. 汲取中外教育精华，坚持综合改革创新

　　人大附中的办学目标是："国内领先，国际一流。""国内领先"，要求我们具备历史的眼光，对中国的教育传统，对中国的教育现状有精深的了解；"国际一流"，要求我们具备世界的眼光，及时掌握别的国家最新的教育思想和教学方法。只有用世界的眼光和历史的眼光看教育，做到知己知彼，经纬交织，我们才能搞清楚世界的教育已发展到了什么水平，中国的基础教育又发展到了什么水平。在此基础上，我们才能做到汲取中外教育精华，坚持综合改革创新。

51. Extract domestic and foreign essence on education, insist on comprehensive reform and innovation

The goal for the development of The High School Affiliated to Renmin University of China is "domestically leading and globally top level". To be "domestically leading" requires us to have a historical vision to deeply understand the tradition and present situation of Chinese education; to be "globally top level" requires us to have a global vision to master the most updated educational theories and methods of other countries in time. Only by using global vision and historical vision to see education, and by knowing both opponent and oneself and learning them horizontally and vertically, shall we figure out what level the global education has developed into, and what the level is of Chinese basic education. Based on this, we would be able to extract domestic and foreign essence on education, and insist on comprehensive reform and innovation.

52. 为中国教育做出最合适的鞋

习近平总书记有句话说得极好，鞋子合不合脚，自己穿了才知道。我们目前最重要的任务，就是为中国教育这双脚做出最合适的鞋。怎样才算最合适？我的理解，一方面，正确处理好古与今的关系，有因有革，返本开新；另一方面，科学处理好中与外的关系，取长补短，洋为中用。我们要在汲取古今中外教育精华的过程中，探索出中国特色社会主义教育现代化之路，这是当代中国教育工作者的历史担当和神圣使命。

52. Make the most suitable shoes for Chinese education

Chairman Xi Jinping once stated a very good point: one only knows whether the shoes are fit after trying them on. Our most important task at the moment is to make the most suitable shoes for the feet which refer to Chinese education. How do you judge whether they are the most suitable? My understanding is that: on one hand, correctly deal with the relationship of history and the present, inherit with reform, and continue the old while investigating the new; on the other hand, we should scientifically deal with the relationship of the domestic and the foreign, learn from each other's strong points and close the gap, and make foreign things serve China. We should explore a modernized socialistic education with Chinese characteristics in the extraction process from domestic and foreign essence. This is the historical responsibility and divine mission of contemporary Chinese educators.

53. 世界教育史是中国教育与欧美教育相互交融的历史

　　中国的科举制度，被誉为指南针、造纸、印刷、火药之后改变历史进程的第五大发明，欧洲的考试制度乃至文官制度，就是从借鉴科举制而来。而近代以来，中国的现代学校制度，则是从欧美传过来。因此，从某种意义上讲，一部世界教育史，也就是中国教育和欧美教育相互交流、相互学习的历史。今天，我们要推动世界教育事业的不断发展，还要坚持这种相互交流、相互学习。

53. The history of global education is one where Chinese and western education blend mutually

The imperial examination system of China is considered as the fifth great invention of ancient China after compass, papermaking technology, typography and gunpowder. The examination system and even system of civil servants in Europe actually used the imperial examination system for reference. And in modern times, modern school systems in China come from the western world. As a result, in a way, the global education history is one where Chinese and western education communicate with and learn from each other. Today, we need to stick to this kind of mutual communication and learning to accelerate the continuous development of the undertaking of world education.

54. 将世界作为我们的教科书

我们不能做一个井底之蛙，不能做一个鼠目寸光、故步自封的人，封闭意味着落后，开放意味着进步。只有将世界作为我们的教科书，我们才会有面向未来的眼光，只有汲取中外教育思想的精华，使之成为我们的精神营养，才能让我们在国内外学校的交流与融合中共同进步。

54. Have the world as our textbook

We can't be like a frog at the bottom of a well, nor a person who just sees an inch of light like a rat and stands too still to make progress. Shutting off means to fall behind, and opening up means to make progress. Only by having the world as our textbook can we have the view to face the future; only by extracting domestic and foreign essence on education and having it as our spiritual nutrition can we make mutual progress in the communication and blending of domestic and foreign schools.

55. 优秀的学校必然是对外开放的学校

　　一所优秀的学校必然是一个对外开放的学校，必然是一个海纳百川、兼收并蓄的学校。一所世界一流的学校，应该是一个能为来自四面八方的年轻人提供受教育机会的国际校园。在这样的校园里，中外教师、学生能在彼此的相互了解中，达到沟通和融合。

55. An excellent school must be one that open up to the world

An excellent school must be one that opens up to the world and must be one that is embracing all and is like a sea where all rivers run into. A world first-class school should be an international campus that allows youngsters from all around the world to have a chance to be educated. In such a campus, domestic and foreign teachers and students would communicate and blend together through mutual understanding.

56. 各国教育应和而不同

最美莫过多样化。我特别欣赏费孝通先生关于世界文明的那四句话："各美其美，美人之美，美美与共，天下大同。"各国的教育，都既有共性，也有个性，应该彼此欣赏，彼此借鉴，春兰秋菊，各擅胜场，在和而不同中共同营造世界教育事业的百花园。

56. Education of different countries should be harmonious but different

Nothing is prettier than diversity. I especially appreciate Mr. Fei Xiaotong's four statements regarding global civilization: "Every form of beauty has its uniqueness. It is precious to appreciate other forms of beauty with openness. If beauty represents itself with diversity and integrity, the world will be blessed with harmony and unity." Education of different countries have their similarities, and their uniqueness. So they should appreciate and mutually learn from each other. Like the orchid in Spring and the chrysanthemum in Autumn, each one has its characteristics, and will jointly construct a garden with a hundred kinds of flowers for the cause of world education.

57.中国基础教育要"引进来，走出去"

中国基础教育已经到了从"引进来"到"走出去"的阶段，我们要深入国外实地去办学，在研究、借鉴国外先进教育教学理念和实践的同时，将中国文化、中国教育在世界各地发扬光大。通过中国基础教育的走出去，让世界听到中国的声音，感受到中国的传统与现代。

57. Chinese basic education should "learn from outside and go global"

Chinese basic education has turned from "learning from outside" to the phase of "going global". We need to really get the foreign territory in the flesh to run schools, and carry Chinese culture and education to other areas of the world, while researching and learning from advanced foreign educational theory and practice. By taking Chinese basic education out, the world would hear the voice of China, and feel the tradition and modernization of China.

人大附中和美国
托马斯杰弗逊理
科高中、美国伊
利诺伊理科高中
联合开展课题
研究

九、艺术、体育与人文社会科学

IX. Art, Physical Education and Humanities and Social Science

58.完整的教育不能缺少艺术教育

艺术可以使人身心和谐、心灵丰富、精神高尚、思维活跃。艺术教育是我们尊重学生个性、开发学生潜能、引导青少年追求美好人生的重要途径，完整的教育不能缺少艺术教育。

58. Education wouldn't be complete without art education

Art can make people feel harmonious both physically and mentally; art can enrich the mind, ennoble the spirit, and activate thoughts. Art education is an important way for us to respect students' personalities, develop their potential and guide them to pursue a beautiful life. Education wouldn't be complete without art education.

艺术之花盛开
——人大附中创新艺术教育模式

59. 美育在学校教育中具有无可替代的重要作用

　　美育是运用人类创造的一切美——音乐、绘画、诗歌，等等——对人自身进行的美的教育，它可以使人心灵丰富，道德完善，思维活跃，身心和谐。美育和德育共同作用于人的精神，引导青少年追求人生的高尚境界和生命的意义与价值。因此，作用于人的心灵和情感的美育必然是素质教育的重要组成部分，在人的教育，特别是学校教育中具有无可替代的重要作用。

59. Education on aesthetics plays an irreplaceable part in school education

　　Education on aesthetics means to use all the beauty created by human beings—such as music, paintings, poetry etc.—to carry out an education to people regarding beauty. It can enrich people's mind, perfect ethics, activate thoughts and harmonious body and heart. Aesthetics and morality education both work on the human mind. They lead young people to pursue a noble status, meaning and value of life. Thus, aesthetics that works on people's minds and emotions must be a significant part of the education for all-round development. It plays an irreplaceable part to education on people, especially for school education.

60.体育是最顶级的教育

　　现代科学研究表明，对婴幼儿、青少年智商的发展，体育运动是最有效的方式之一。有的学者甚至认为，体育是最顶级的教育，我对此深以为然。这是因为，体育除了培育学生的身体健康、运动技能外，更是在培养学生的意志品质、创造力、心理素质、德行修养以及提升生命和生活质量方面具有不可或缺的重要作用。

60. P.E. is the top-level education

Modern scientific research shows that, physical education is one of the most effective ways to develop IQ for infants and teenagers. Some scholars even believe that P.E. is the top-level education, and I totally agree with it. Besides training students' physical health and athletic skills, P.E. also plays an indispensable role in raising children with volitional qualities, creativity, psychological qualities and moral accomplishment, as well as improving life and living quality.

61. 培养"三高"体育后备人才

"道德品质高、文化素质高、运动水平高"的"三高"理念，是人大附中创新教育思想的产物，也是我们为国家培养优秀体育后备人才的理想目标。为此我们开创了半训半读的体教结合模式，它可以让学生不因参加体育训练而荒废学业，即便不能进入体育人才金字塔的塔尖也仍然会有出路；同时，又可以普遍提高在校学生中少年运动员的文化素养，为职业队和国家队输送综合素质良好的高水平体育后备人才。

61. Cultivate talents in sports with "three excellences" as talent reserve

The "three excellences" means "excellent moral quality, excellent literacy, and excellent athletic levels". It's the product of the innovative education concept of The High School Affiliated to Renmin University of China, and it's our ideal to raise excellent talents in sports for our country. For this we created the P.E. education model combining half training with half schooling. It allows students not to abandon schooling because of physical training, but still have an option even if they can't reach the spire of sport talent pyramid; meanwhile, this model can generally improve the literacy of the young athletics that are still in school, and thus provide high-level talents in sports with good comprehensive quality for professional sports teams and the national team.

飞翔的"三高"
——人大附中
"三高"足球队

62. 艺术教育和体育要推进普及与提高相结合

学校艺术教育和体育首先要面向全体学生，培养所有学生的艺术和运动素养，使他们身心和谐、意志坚毅、情操高尚、趣味高雅；同时也要为具有各类艺术特长和体育特长的孩子搭建平台，让他们的才华得到充分发展，这应该成为学校教育追求的理想境界。

62. We should keep facilitating the combination of popularizing and enhancing in terms of art education and P.E.

Art and physical education in school should first face all students to cultivate their art and sports qualities, making them harmonious both physically and mentally, and nurturing their strong will, noble sentiment, and fine interests; in the meantime, we should establish a platform for the children who have all kinds of art or sports specialties to fully develop their talents. This should be the ideal status for schools to pursue in education.

63. 基础教育要加强人文社会科学教育

人文社会科学的重要性不言而喻，在基础教育领域加强人文社会科学教育是当前我国基础教育改革的一个重要课题。概括来说，人文社会科学对青少年具有以下四方面的重要意义：一是人文社会科学能促进思想解放，激发创新思维；二是人文社会科学能将经验提炼为理论，知识升华为智慧，从而使人站得高、看得远、想得深、干得准，达到"登高壮观天地间"的境界；三是人文社会科学的内核是科学的世界观、人生观、价值观，是对真善美的追求，这是人之所以为人的根本，也是教育工作的根本出发点和落脚点；四是人文社会科学的魅力就在于"人文精神"和"人文关怀"。

63. In basic education, humanities and social sciences should be reinforced

It goes without saying about the importance of humanities and social sciences. Strengthening humanities and social science education in basic education is a substantial project for the reform of basic education in our country. Generally speaking, humanities and social sciences have the following four significant meanings for youngsters: firstly, humanities and social sciences can facilitate ideological emancipation, and inspire innovative ideas; secondly, humanities and social sciences can abstract theory from experience, and elevate knowledge into wisdom so that people would stand higher, look farther, think deeper, act more accurately and finally reach the state of "watching everything of the world from the top"; thirdly, the core of humanities and social sciences is a scientific world view, outlook on life and value system, and is the pursuit for the true, the good and the beautiful. It's the essence of the human nature, and it's the fundamental starting point and foothold of education; fourthly, the charm of humanities and social sciences lies in "humanistic spirit" and "humanistic concern".

64. 人文社会科学教育培养"靠得住"的人

　　我们推进素质教育，到底要培养什么样的人？我想用六个字来概括，那就是"有本事，靠得住"。"有本事"好理解，什么是"靠得住"呢？就是有伟大的理想、高尚的人格、健全的心理，能将自己的本事用于服务祖国、造福人类。后者需要在基础教育阶段加强人文社会科学教育，让他们在饱览人文社科的波澜壮阔、独立思考内化之后，将自身的命运与国家、民族、人类的命运联系在一起，成为一个大写的人。

64. The education of humanities and social science nurtures people who are "reliable"

When we implement education for all-round development, what kind of people do we want to cultivate exactly? I think it can be summarized into 2 words: "capable, reliable". "Capable" is easy to understand, then what is "reliable"? It means one has great ambition, a noble personality, a sound mentality, and can use his capabilities to serve his motherland and benefit mankind. In order to achieve the latter, we should reinforce the education of humanities and social sciences in the phase of basic education to give students a chance of full access to the magnificent upsurge of humanities and social sciences, as well as internalizing an independent thinking, so that afterwards they would tie their fates with the country, nation and humankind to become a real man.

65. 阅读与写作是每一个人都需具备的基本技能

　　我希望我们学校的每一个学生都能够读很多好书，写一手好文章，做一个能干能说能写，既善于表达自己又能够理解他人的人。阅读和写作是如此的重要，无论对自身的修养和生活，还是从事科研活动、办企业等，都离不开它们。

65. Reading and writing is the basic skill that everyone should possess

I hope every student in our school would read a lot of good books and can be good at writing; be a man that excels at doing, speaking and writing; be a person that can not only express himself well, but also is capable of understanding others. Reading and writing are so important that they can work on personal accomplishment and life, science research activities and business management.

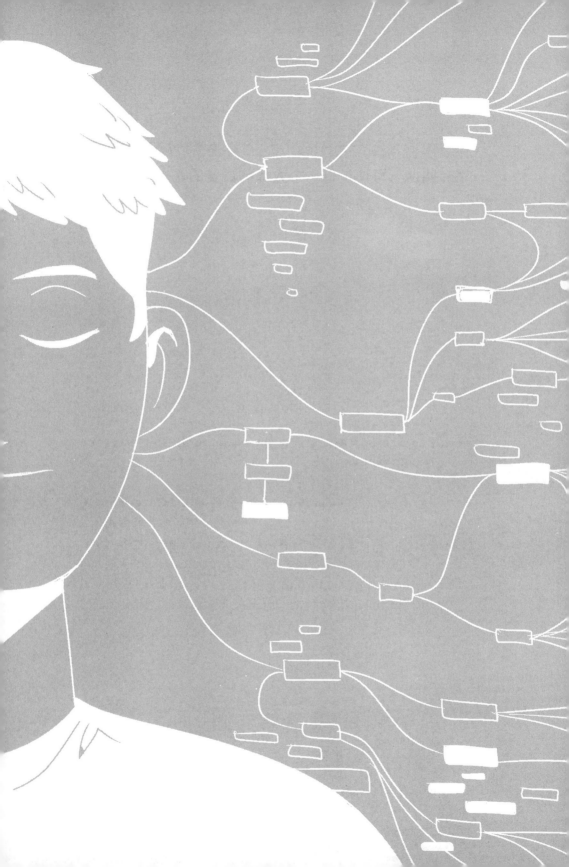

十、科学教育

X. Science Education

66. 科学教育要从娃娃抓起

　　科学教育是现代学校教育的重要组成部分，然而我国的幼儿园、中小学在这方面还很欠缺。科学教育所涉及的是与之相关联的一系列精神与技能，它需要、也必须从小抓起：一是要培养孩子的科学精神，二是要培养孩子的科学素养，三是要科学教育与实践相结合，四是要在基础教育阶段形成小学、初中、高中相衔接的科学教育体系。

66. Science education shall start from kids

Science education is a critical composition of modern school education, yet the kindergarten, elementary and secondary schools in our country are rather lacking in this area. Science education involves a series of spirits and skills related to it, so it needs to and has to begin with kids: firstly we should cultivate the scientific spirit for the kids; secondly we should raise them with scientific quality; thirdly science education should be combined with practice; fourthly we should form a system that can connect primary schools, junior and senior high schools in science education along the phase of basic education.

67. 中学要为学生提供科研的实践训练

中国的发展需要大量的科学研究人才，他们的自主创新能力，他们对科研的热情与执着，他们坚实的研究素养，和国家的全面、协调、可持续发展密切相关。而这些，离不开青少年时期的引导与培养。尤其是在中学这一关键期，学校要提供机会让学生们得到科研的实践训练，使他们的科研热情和科研素质得到良好的挖掘和发展。

67. Secondary school should offer students practical trainings on scientific research

China's development requires a huge quantity of manpower on scientific research. Their capability on indigenous innovation, their passion and persistence to scientific research, their solid researching quality, all tie closely to the full, coordinated and sustainable development of the country. And this can't be achieved without the guidance and development in the youth period. Especially in such a critical period, middle schools should provide students an opportunity to get practical training on scientific research, and progress well and develop their passion and quality in scientific research.

68. 中学开展科学教育要求教师具备科学素养 和科研能力

　　当人大附中引进第一个博士教师时，有人质疑这是对人才的浪费。随着我国基础教育阶段对创新和科研的重视，越来越多的学校开始不断引进经过严格科研训练的博士教师，这是因为，中学要开展科学教育，必须要有具备科学素养和科研能力的教师进行指导，靠学生自己摸索是不行的。这也是我国日渐进入基础教育发达国家的一个标志。

68. It requires teachers to have scientific qualities and researching capabilities if secondary school wants to extend science education

When The High School Affiliated to Renmin University of China recruited the first teacher with a doctorate degree, some people doubted that this would be a waste of talent. As the basic education in our country focuses more and more on innovation and scientific research, more and more schools start to recruit teachers with doctorate degrees who have received strict training on scientific research. This is because, if a secondary school wants to extend science education, it must have teachers with scientific qualities and researching capabilities to guide them, and it won't work if students merely study on their own. This is to mark that China has gradually entered the line of countries with developed basic education.

69. 科学研究是学校教育的内在驱动力

　　科学技术是第一生产力。我认为，对于学校教育来说，科学研究也是其内在驱动力。很难想象，一个没有科研氛围和科研奖励机制的学校，会在学校教育的各个方面取得喜人的成绩。实际上，科学研究是一只隐形的手，它在无形中推动着学校教育的发展。我们要摈弃当前影响中小学教育科研改革的"教育科研神秘观，教育科研恐惧观，教育科研名利观"，切实走科研兴校、校兴科研之路。

69. Scientific research is the internal power of school education

Science and technology constitutes a primary productive force. I think for school education, scientific research is the internal driving force. It's hard to imagine a school without a scientific research atmosphere and rewarding system which would achieve remarkable results in various aspects of school education. In fact, scientific research is an invisible hand that can imperceptibly push the educational development of the school. We should banish the concepts that affect the scientific reform of elementary and secondary schools like "the hiding of educational scientific research from others, the fear of educational scientific research, and educational scientific research for fame and wealth", and actually walk on the path that "scientific research helps a school flourish, and a school will make scientific research thrive".

70. 科学教育与艺术教育相结合培养学生的创造力

很多伟大的科学家也是超群的艺术家。艺术能激发一个人的灵感和创造性，科学教育与艺术教育相结合，能够在愉悦学生身心的同时，为他们插上创造的翅膀，迸发出无尽的创造力。

70. Combine science and art education to cultivate the creativity of students

Many great scientists are outstanding artists at the same time. Art can stimulate one's inspiration and creativity. The combination of science and art education can provide physical and mental pleasure to students, while giving them the wings of creation and bursting out infinite creativity.

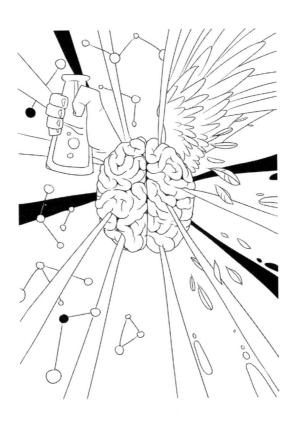

十一、现代教育技术

XI. Modern Educational Technology

71. 现代教育技术带来的是教育教学全方位的改变与进步

　　对现代教育技术在教育教学中的运用，应该有全新的认识，它带来的已不仅仅是教学手段的更新，而是教育理念、教育内容、教育形式、教育效益的全面进步。未来教育，在时空上都会与过去、现在大不相同，谁拒绝现代教育技术在教育教学中的运用，谁就将被时代所抛弃。

71. Modern educational technology brings an all-around change and advancement in educating and teaching

For the application of modern educational technology in educating and teaching, we should have a brand new understanding. It not only brings in an update on teaching methods, but also an overall progress on educational concepts, contents, forms and effectiveness. Future education will differ from that of the past or present in both space and time. Those who refuse to apply modern educational technology in education and teaching shall be phased out by that time.

72. 教育工作者要让现代教育技术成为教育发展的助跑器

　　跨越时空的数字化教学，将成为 21 世纪的重要教学方式，对促进教育发展、实现教育公平、构建终身教育体系和建设学习型社会具有不可替代的革命性作用。一个只会使用粉笔和黑板的教师将会被时代淘汰。教育工作者也要与时俱进，让现代教育技术成为教育发展的助跑器。

72. Educators should embrace modern educational technology to be the run-up device for the education development

The digital teaching that runs across space and time will be an important teaching method in the 21st century. It has an irreplaceable revolution-like impact on improving education development, achieving education equity, establishing lifelong education systems, and constructing a learning-inclined society. A teacher who is only capable of using chalk and blackboards will be eliminated by that time. Educators should also keep up with the time, having modern educational technology boost education development.

73. 以教育的信息化带动教育的现代化

在信息愈来愈发达的今天，谁拥有一流的信息资源，并有效地利用好这一资源，谁就能在竞争中处于有利地位。信息这种古老而又崭新的"资源"，与物质、能源并驾齐驱，已成为决定未来社会发展的重要财富。要实现基础教育的跨越式发展，必须以教育的信息化带动教育的现代化，创建以电脑网络为基础，以图书馆为信息源，以数字化为模式，以现代教育技术为手段的现代化教学环境。

73. Use the advanced information technology in education to drive the modernization of education

In today's world where information becomes more and more flourishing, the one who owns first-class information resources and makes effective use of them shall gain the upper hand in the competition. Information, the old yet brand new "resource", has become a substantial treasure that can determine the development of future societies along with materials and energy. In order to make a grand development of basic education, we must use the advanced information technology in education to drive the modernization of education: create a modern teaching environment with computers and internet as the foundation, with libraries as the information source, with digitalization as the model and with modern educational technology as methods.

74. 人工智能将带来教育教学翻天覆地的变化

　　教师可不可能被人工智能所取代？不能。但这只是指人格、道德这些非教育教学内容的部分。随着人工智能的高速发展，可以预见，在不久的将来，一些原本由每个教师亲力亲为的工作都将被取代。教师得以从繁重的琐事中解脱出来，为每个学生提供"传道，授业，解惑"的有针对性的服务。

74. AI will bring earth-shaking changes to educating and teaching

Can teachers be replaced by AI? No. But this only refers to the non-teaching-content like personality and morality. With the high-speed development of AI, it can be predicted that in the near future, some work that formerly requires each teacher to carry out, shall be replaced. Teachers will be released from heavy trivial matters and be able to provide pertinent services like "teaching principles, instructing skills, and removing doubts" to every student.

十二、家庭教育

XII. Family Education

75. 家庭教育与学校教育都应以爱与尊重为前提

　　家庭教育与学校教育之间没有本质的不同。尤其是在当今思想、经济、文化等均多元共存，青少年一代大量接受各种资讯、寻求人格独立与精神自主的情况下，无论是学科教学还是道德、心理健康教育，学校教育都必须摒弃原有的简单说教、灌输方式，家庭教育也必须改变原有的家长制作风，以民主、开放、包容的心态去对待学生、对待孩子。不管是家长还是老师，都应该以爱和尊重来打开孩子的心扉、激发孩子的潜能、促进他们的成长与成才。

75. Love and respect should be put as the precondition in family and school education

Family education has no essential difference from school education. Especially in current times when diversity coexists in fields like thought, the economy and culture, and the younger generation receives massive information and seeks independence on personality and spirit. Under such circumstances, schools should abandon the previous simple ways of lecturing or inculcation in subject teaching or moral and mental health education, whereas family education should also change the patriarchy style and treat students and children with a democratic, open and tolerating mind. Both parents and teachers should try to open children's minds and inspire their potential to promote their growth and success with love and respect.

76. 家庭教育作为第一课堂具有更为重要的作用

　　谈到教育，大多数人马上想到的是学校教育。学校教育固然重要，但更多地体现在知识传承、技能培养上，就人格塑造、道德养成、身心健康、情绪情感这些方面而言，家庭教育作为第一课堂则具有更为重要、不可替代的作用，其影响贯穿一个生命体的始终。

76. As the first learning experience, family education plays a more important role

　　Speaking of education, most people would immediately think of school education. As important as school education is, it acts more by passing on knowledge and training skills. In terms of character building, morality formation, physical and mental health as well as sentiments and emotions, family education plays a more important and irreplaceable role as the first learning experience, and its influence will run through one's entire life.

77. 家庭教育从教育家长开始

合格的、优秀的家长不是天然形成的，也需要为他们提供合适的教育。学校、政府、社会应形成合力，为每一个家长提供家庭教育的相关知识与技能，这对当今的中国社会尤为重要。

77. Family education starts with the educating of parents

People are not born a qualified and excellent parent, so they need to be provided with proper education. Schools, governments, and the society shall form a joint force to provide each parent with related knowledge and skills on family education. This is especially important for the current society of China.

78. 解放孩子是家庭教育的要义所在

　　解放孩子，将孩子看成一个独立的、有自己思想和行动力的人，是当今家庭教育的要义所在。这种解放，是相对"桎梏"、"控制"而言的，解放孩子，就是要让孩子在成长中释放天性，成为他自己。一个人只有首先成为一个独立自主的个体，才能在心理上、精神上积极主动地探索世界、拥抱生命、对自己对他人对社会负责，在从事自己喜欢和有意义的事情中实现价值、造福社会，过幸福的人生。

78. To set children free is the essence of family education

To set children free, and to treat them as an independent person with their own mind and actions, are the essence of family education in today's world. Comparatively speaking, this kind of freedom is contrary to "shackle" and "control". To set children free is to free their nature and let them be themselves. Only by becoming an independent individual shall one person be able to psychologically, mentally and actively explore the world, embrace life, and be responsible for themselves, for others and for the society; one can achieve values, do well for the society and lead a happy life by doing the things they love and things that are meaningful.

十三、创新人才培养

XIII. Cultivation of Innovative Talents

79. 培养创新人才是我们的责任和快乐

中国的青少年禀赋之好、潜能之大、创造欲望之强烈、创造能力之杰出，大大超出我们的意料。他们在研究性学习和发明创造中表现出来的独立自主意识、团结协作精神、社会责任感和锲而不舍的毅力，更让我们感动和钦佩。培养学生的创新精神和实践能力，既是我们的责任，更是我们的快乐。

人大附中探索拔
尖创新人才早期
培养模式试验项
目掠影

79. Cultivating innovative talents is our responsibility and happiness

It is far beyond our expectations that Chinese teenagers have such good gifts, big potential and strong desires and outstanding abilities in creation. The independent consciousness, spirit of teamwork, social responsibility, and persistent willpower reflected in their research-based learning and innovative creation are moving and deeply admired. Cultivating students with a spirit of innovation and capability to practice is not only our duty, but also our happiness.

80. 教育工作者应是一个"发现者"和"点火者"

　　每个人都有创新的潜力，或大或小。教育工作者应该是一个"发现者"——发现每个学生身上的潜质和特点，有了发现，培养才会事半功倍；教育工作者应该是一个"点火者"——点燃每个学生体内蕴藏的能量，他的重要职责是通过"点火"让学生的能量充分发挥出来；教育工作者应该是一个理想主义者和完美主义者——让每一个学生都能在全面发展的基础上各有特长。教育工作者必须有这样的境界和追求。

80. Educators should be "discoverers" and "fire lighters"

　　Each one has potential to innovate, it is just a matter of how big or small that potential is. Educators should be a "discoverer"— find the potential and features of every student. Only by discovering students potential will training yield twice the result with half the effort; educators should be a "fire lighter"—light up the energy within each student. The most important responsibility is to fully bring out students' energy; educators should be idealists and perfectionists— let every student identify their own strengths on the basis of overall development. Educators must have such a vision and pursuit.

81. 教育要处理好"共同发展"和"特殊发展"的关系

　　正确处理好"共同发展"和"特殊发展"的关系，将"有教无类"的博爱精神和"因材施教"的科学方法有机地结合起来，避免有的学生"吃不饱"、有的学生"吃不了"的现象。人的创造性思维有强有弱，人的创新能力有大有小，这是客观事实。正视这个事实，就要在培养全体学生创新精神和创新能力的基础上，对一些有独特潜能的学生进行特殊教育，这才是对每个学生负责的实事求是的态度。

81. The relationship between "mutual development" and "special development" should be handled well

Handling the relationship between "mutual development" and "special development" correctly, and organically combining the "no child left behind" spirit of big love and scientific method like "teaching students in accordance with their aptitude" will avoid situations where some students "are on short rations" while some "have too much to eat". Different people have different levels of innovative thinking skills, and their innovative capability could differ from one another. This is the objective fact. We shall face it squarely and provide some students with special potentials with particular education on the basis of the cultivation of innovative spirit and capability for all students. Such ways are the practical, truthful and responsible attitude we should have for every single student.

82.给孩子的想象力施肥浇水

如果说好奇心是孩子打开未知世界的钥匙，想象力就是孩子探索和创造一个新世界的能力。这种能力是一种智慧，它不同于知识，知识只能看到一块石头就是一块石头，一粒沙子就是一粒沙子，智慧却能在一块石头里看见风景，在一粒沙子中发现灵魂。每个孩子都有丰富的想象力，呵护他，鼓励他，给他的想象施肥浇水，也许在想象萌发的地方就会长出创造的大树。

82. Fertilize and water children's imagination

If curiosity is the key for kids to open the door to the unknown world, imagination is the power for them to explore and create a new world. This capability is a kind of wisdom. Unlike knowledge which can only see a stone as a stone, and a grain of sand as sand, wisdom can see landscape out of a stone, and discover soul from a grain of sand. Every child has a rich imagination. By caring for him, encouraging him, as well as fertilizing and watering his imagination, a big tree of innovation will grow out of the place where his imagination sprouts.

人大附中早培
班：体会关爱，
共同成长

83. 问题意识是创新人才培养的一把"金钥匙"

　　学问学问，"学"必须与"问"连在一起，而且"问"是学问的发动机。人类社会就是在不断地发现问题、回答问题、解决问题中进步的。创新人才，首先是善于发现问题的人才，而且是善于在众多问题中发现核心问题的人才。所有创新人才都是"问题中人"，没有问题，就没有创新。发现并解决了小问题，便成就了小创新；发现并解决了大问题，便成就了大创新。中学培养创新人才，一定要鼓励孩子善于发现问题、敢于提出问题，一定要培养孩子在回答问题、解决问题过程中的专心致志、锲而不舍。问题意识，是创新人才培养的一把"金钥匙"。

83. Problem consciousness is a "golden key" for the cultivation of innovative talents

For knowledge, one must connect "learning" with "inquiring", and "inquiring" is the motor of knowledge. Human society makes its progress in the continuous process of discovering, answering and solving problems. An innovative talent should first be a person who's good at discovering problems, and be one that can figure out a critical problem out of many. All innovative talents are "people with problems". There shall be no innovation without problems. The discovery and the solving of a small problem make a small innovation; and the discovery and the solving of a big problem makes a big innovation. To cultivate innovative talents, a secondary school must encourage children to be good at the discovery of problems and daring to raise it; we must cultivate children to stay focused and be persistent in the process of answering and solving problems. Problem consciousness is a "golden key" for the cultivation of innovative talents.

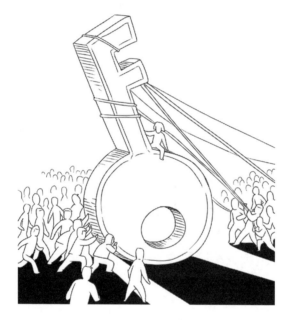

84. 中学培养创新人才要培养孩子的团队精神

面向未来、面向世界、面向现代化，我们在鼓励孩子独立思考的同时，要高度重视培养孩子的协同精神。"协同创新"已成为当代创新的主要形式，也是当代创新能最终成功、能产生巨大效益的根本保证。中学培养创新人才，必须认清这种趋势，顺应这种趋势，从娃娃抓起，培养孩子的团队精神。

84. Secondary schools should cultivate children's teamwork spirit while raising innovative talents

While facing the future, facing the world, and facing modernization, we encourage children to think independently; at the same time, we should attach great importance to cultivating their sense of collaboration. "Collaborative innovation" is already a main form of modern innovation, as well as the fundamental guarantee for modern innovation to eventually succeed and generate huge benefit. While cultivating innovative talents, middle schools must be aware of this trend and comply with it, and cultivate children's teamwork spirit starting from kids.

85. 中学培养创新人才要"减负、增趣"

　　培养创新人才必须与"减负"同步。因为对于青少年来说，负担减轻了，身体才会放松，心境才会空灵。唯如此，好奇心、想象力才能长出翅膀，自由飞翔。而好奇心、想象力是一切创新的基础。但"减负"的目的不是"放羊"，"减负"的目的是为了孩子更好的成长。因此，"减负"的同时还要"增趣"，学校要开设大量选修课，成立各种各样的学生社团、课题小组、项目小组、兴趣小组，让孩子快快乐乐地动手动脑，高高兴兴地做事做人。"减负"与"增趣"同步，有减有增、减增适宜，是培养创新人才的有效途径，这中间的关键是真正让中小学生自主地学习、快乐地学习，真正让中小学生把时间和精力投放在应该投放的地方。

85. Secondary schools should "alleviate burden" and "increase fun" while cultivating innovative talents

The cultivation of innovative talents must be synchronized with "alleviating burdens". Because for teenagers, they only have physical and mental relaxation and a flexible and elusive mind after the alleviation of their burdens. Only through this will their curiosity and imagination grow wings and fly freely. Curiosity and imagination are the basis for all innovation. But the goal of "alleviating burdens" is not "to be free without limit", but to have children enjoy better growth. Therefore, we should "alleviate burdens" and in the meantime, "increase fun". Schools should offer abundant elective courses, and establish all kinds of student clubs, research teams, project teams and interest groups so that children can happily think and practice, as well as do things and grow up in joy. Synchronizing "alleviating burdens" with "increasing fun" means to have proper increase and decrease at the same time. It's an effective way to cultivate innovative talents. The key of it all is to let students in elementary and secondary schools truly study actively and happily, and let them spend their time and energy in the correct place.

86.培养拔尖创新人才应站在国家战略的高度

　　进入新世纪，国与国之间的竞争，越来越集中体现于人才的竞争；人才的竞争越来越集中体现于拔尖创新人才的竞争。对此，我们一定要有清醒认识，一定要有只争朝夕的紧迫感，一定要尽快形成拔尖创新人才培养的国家战略。拔尖创新人才培养的国家战略，毫无疑问，应该涵盖从高等教育到基础教育等各个学段、各个环节。

86. We should stand from the national perspective to cultivate top-notch innovative talents

After entering the new century, the competition between countries is demonstrated more and more through the competition of talents; and the competition of talents more and more centers around the competition of top-notch innovative talents. We must clearly recognize this and must have a sense of urgency that the clock is ticking, and a national strategy of cultivating top-notch innovative talents must be developed as soon as possible. This national strategy on cultivating top-notch innovative talents should no doubt cover all schooling stages and all links from advanced education to basic education.

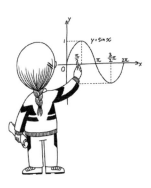

87."无为而治"在培养拔尖创新人才上更为重要

　　我们仔细研究古今中外的拔尖创新人才成长史，可以发现这样一个规律：拔尖创新人才几乎都不是刻意培养出来的，而是在良好的教育和社会环境中自然成长起来的。因此，在培养拔尖创新人才上，无为而治往往更重要。所谓无为而治，不是真的无所作为，而是一种哲学意义上的自觉的无为。培养拔尖创新人才上的无为而治，从政府层面上讲，就是给学校放权，扩大学校的自主权，让校长们解放思想，开动脑筋，大胆地试，大胆地闯；从学校层面上讲，就是进一步减轻学生的课业负担，进一步创造宽松的教学环境，让学生的天性得到自由发展，让学生的特长得到充分展现。这两个层面的无为而治做到了，拔尖创新人才才可能崭露头角，才可能被发现，教育工作者才能真正有所作为，才能用特殊的载体和特殊的方法，因材施教，从而按教育规律办事，按人才成长规律办事。

87. "Governing by doing nothing that goes against nature" is more important on the cultivation of top-notch innovative talents

When we research deep into the growing history of top-notch innovative talents at all times and in all countries, we can discover the following pattern: top-notch innovative talents are not cultivated through a designed and set path, but through natural growth within a good educational and social environment. Therefore, to cultivate top-notch innovative talents, "governing by doing nothing that goes against nature" is more important. "Governing by doing nothing that goes against nature" doesn't actually mean do nothing, but a philosophical and deliberate use of inaction . "Governing by doing nothing that goes against nature" in cultivating top-notch innovative talents, on the government scale, means to delegate power to schools, and extend schools' decision making, as well as liberating principals' concerns so they can set their wits to work, dare to try and dare to be adventurous; on the school scale, it means to keep reducing students' work load, keep creating a tolerant teaching environment so that students' natural instincts can be developed freely, and their specialty can be fully shown. Only when we make these 2 principles on both scales will top-notch innovative talents emerge and can be possibly discovered; meanwhile educators can finally make a difference, can use special support and methods to teach students in accordance with their aptitude, so that the patterns of education and the patterns that facilitate talent growth will be followed.

88. 拔尖创新人才要从小发现、从小培养

　　拔尖创新人才是一个国家的核心竞争力，需要从小发现、从小培养，这些人才在 20 岁之前就应该完成基础教育阶段的教育，并在某些领域初露端倪。人的天赋与才能存在差异，有的孩子智力超常，有的孩子有文艺、体育天赋，有的孩子具有发明创造潜能，"人生天地间，各自有禀赋"。大自然中每棵树不可能长得一样高，每朵花的颜色不可能完全相同，自然规律如此，学生发展的规律也不例外。应当是"立脚点上求平等，于出头处谋自由"，基础教育既要对学生"求平等"，也要为孩子个性潜能的充分发展"谋自由"。

88. Top-notch innovative talents should be discovered when little and cultivated from an early age

Top-notch innovative talents are the core competitiveness of a country, and they need to be discovered and cultivated from early ages. These talents should finish basic education before 20 years old, and show some gifts in certain fields. The talent and capability of people differ from each other. Some children have gifted intelligence, some are gifted in arts and sports, and some have the potential for inventions and creation. "People are born into this world with different gifts." In nature, it is not possible for all trees to grow to the same height, and not possible for flowers to have the same color. This is the law of nature, and the law on students' development makes no exception. We should "make equality on foothold, and give freedom to the result". Basic education not only requires "equality" for students, but also asks for "freedom" for the full development of children on character and potential.

89. 拔尖创新人才早期培养要上下互动、左右联动

拔尖创新人才的早期培养，必须上有政府支持、下有学校实践，必须小学、中学、大学全线贯通，这就是上下互动。拔尖创新人才的早期培养，必须是所有有条件的学校一起努力、达成共识、形成合力，这就是左右联动。上下互动、左右联动，才能良性循环。这种良性循环形成之日，就是中国的大批拔尖创新人才出头之日。

89. The early stage cultivation on top-notch innovative talents should have "up-down interaction" and "left-right linkage"

The early stage cultivation of top-notch innovative talents must have support from the upper side-the government, and practice from schools. It also requires a full line-up of work by elementary schools, secondary schools and universities. This is the "up-down interaction". The early stage cultivation of top-notch innovative talents must provide all schools with the conditions to work together, form common views and finally reach a joint force. This is the "left-right linkage". Only with "up-down interaction" and "left-right linkage", shall we achieve a beneficial cycle. The day this cycle is formed, is the day where a big batch of top-notch innovative talents shall emerge.

90. 素质教育的关键在于培养学生的创新精神和
实践能力

　　如果说实施素质教育就像烧一壶开水的话，培养学生的创新精神和实践能力做不好，这壶水就永远是六七十度，永远开不了；如果说实施素质教育就像画一条龙的话，培养学生的创新精神和实践能力就是点睛之笔，没有点睛之笔，这条龙就活不起来、飞不起来。素质教育这篇大文章能不能写好、能不能出彩，关键就在能否培养学生的创新精神和实践能力上，关键就在能否培养更多拔尖创新人才上。

90. The key of the education for all-round development is to nurture students to have a spirit of innovation and ability to practice

If we compare the education for all-round development to boiling a pot of hot water, then the water would never be boiled but always stay in 60–70°C once we fail to cultivate students with a spirit of innovation and ability to practice; and if we compare the education for all-round development to drawing a dragon, then the cultivation of a spirit of innovation and ability to practice is the finishing touch without which the dragon won't come alive nor fly. The key to write the article of the education for all-round development well and splendid lies in whether we can cultivate students with a spirit of innovation and ability to practice, in whether we can cultivate more top innovative talents.

十四、教育均衡

XIV. Education Equilibrium

91. 整个教育事业是一所学校的大生命

　　人的生命有大小之分，小生命蕴含在自己的身体内，大生命则体现在人群和社会中；一所学校的生命也有大小之分，小生命则蕴含在自己的校园内，大生命则体现在整个教育事业中。

91. The entire education undertaking is the "big life" of the school

　　Human Life consists of a "Big Life" and a "Small Life". The "Small Life" is implied within one's own body, and the "Big Life" is reflected within people and societies; The life of a school consists of a "Big Life" and a "Small Life" as well, The "Small Life" is implied within the own school, and the "Big Life" is reflected within the cause of education.

92. 优质学校不仅要"独善其身"，还要"兼济天下"

一所示范校的意义，不仅在于它自身发展得有多好，而且还在于它发挥了多大的示范和辐射作用。优质学校的校长要有"忧国忧民忧天下"的情怀，不仅要"独善其身"，还要"兼济天下"。让更多的学校分享优质学校的教学资源，让更多的学校借鉴优质学校的办学经验，帮助更多的薄弱学校提高水平，这才是更高境界地履行社会责任。

92. An excellent school should not only "pay attention to one's own development without thinking of others", but also "make the world a better place"

The meaning of a demonstrative school not only shows how well it develops, but also how much it serves as a model and an example. The principal of an excellent school should have the noble sentiment of "caring for the country, for the people and the world"; he should not only "pay attention to one's own development without thinking of others", but also "make the world a better place". It is fulfilling social responsibilities on a higher scale for excellent schools to share educational resources and share school operation experiences in order to help more weak schools to improve.

93. 让更多孩子享受优质教育是教育均衡的终极目标

共和国的每一个孩子，无论富贵贫穷，无论身处城市乡村，都有享受优质教育的权利，都有通过教育改变命运的梦想。促进教育均衡就是要让更多孩子享受优质教育，让更多教师成为优秀教师，让更多校长成为优秀校长，让更多学校成为人民满意的学校。

93. The ultimate goal of education equilibrium is to have more children enjoy the education for all-round development

Each one of the children in our country, rich or poor, in cities or in rural areas, all have the right to enjoy the education for all-round development, and have a dream to change their lives through education. Promoting education equilibrium is to let more children enjoy the education for all-round development, for more teachers to become excellent, for more principals to become outstanding, and more schools to become ones that people are satisfied with.

94. 素质教育和教育均衡是我国成为教育强国的两大标志

　　中国教育要迈上新台阶、进入新境界，一要靠素质教育，二要靠教育均衡。素质教育搞好了，教育发展均衡了，这是我们由教育大国变成教育强国的两大标志。

94. The two signs that our country has become a strong nation in education are the education for all-round development and education equilibrium

If Chinese education is to advance and enter a new realm, we first need to count on education for all-round development, and then count on education equilibrium. Once the education for all-round development is well carried out, and the development of education has become balanced, then these are the two signs that our country has become a strong nation in education.

95. 发展中学教育要"下要保底，上不封顶"

　　发展中学教育，要坚持公平优先、兼顾效率的原则。建议在政策上"下要保底，上不封顶"。"下要保底"，指一定要保证每个孩子都平等享受符合国家标准的义务教育；"上不封顶"，指对现有各方面工作都做得比较好的优质中学，要鼓励其保持优势、继续发展、不断超越，成为中学教育的品牌学校，并充分发挥品牌学校的示范作用、辐射作用，带动整个中学教育水平的提高。"下要保底，上不封顶"，基本要求就是薄弱校不薄弱，优质校更优质；最终目标就是教育水平的整体提高。

95. The development of secondary school education should "give minimum guarantee, but set no ceiling limit"

The development of secondary school education should insist on principles that equality comes first and efficiency must be considered. For policies, I would suggest to "give minimum guarantee, but set no ceiling limit". "Give minimum guarantee", means to guarantee that every child will equally have a compulsory education that fits national standards; "set no ceiling limit" means for excellent middle schools that do all kinds of work well, we should encourage them to keep the advantage, keep developing and keep surpassing, and become the brand schools of secondary school education. These schools should act as a model and radiating function of brand schools and drives the overall improvement of secondary school levels. The basic requirement of "giving minimum guarantee, but setting no ceiling limit" is that weak schools are not weak anymore, but excellent schools become better; the ultimate goal is to achieve an overall improvement on education level.

96. 教育公平不是削峰填谷

教育公平不是削峰填谷、"劫富济贫"。我们要为品牌中学创造宽松的环境，不能"木秀于林，风必摧之"。强校更强，弱校不弱，强校办分校、助弱校，实现基础教育的优质均衡发展。

96. Education equilibrium doesn't mean de-peaking

Education equilibrium doesn't mean de-peaking, nor "robbing the rich to help the poor". We should create a tolerant environment for brand secondary schools instead of "when one tree grows outstanding it would definitely attract destruction from the wind". We should let strong schools become stronger, and weak schools become better; strong schools open branch schools and help weak schools to achieve an excellent and balanced development on basic education.

97. 优质校"帮一所成一所"的要诀是派去管理型"打鱼人"

　　优质校在帮扶薄弱校、开办分校的过程中，如何真正实现"帮一所成一所、办一所成一所"？我们的经验是：授人以鱼不如授人以渔，授人以渔不如派去带领打鱼的人。派出管理型的"打鱼人"，既避免了大规模输出教师的负担，也能手把手带领、孵化出一批"卓越教师"与"卓越校长"，提升当地学校的发展气质。更重要的是，这样的模式也能"反哺"本校。外派教师、干部在干事创业中提升了教学经验和管理能力，骨干调离、年轻教师补缺的方式，也让人才梯队更高效地成长起来。名校不仅不会被"掏空"，反而能越做越大，这就是"赠人玫瑰，手有余香"。

我们的课堂在一起——人大附中教育帮扶案例："双师教学"

97. The critical point for excellent schools to do "help one to make one" is to send a "fisherman" of administrative type

In the process of assisting weak schools and opening branch schools, how can an excellent school really make "help one to make one, open one to succeed one" happen? Our experience is: teaching one how to fish instead of just giving fish, but sending a fisherman to lead them fish is better than teaching one how to fish. By sending out a "fisherman" of administrative type, we can avoid the burden to send out a big amount of teachers, but can lead and help them hand in hand to hatch a batch of "remarkable teachers" and "outstanding headmasters", and improve their developing temperament. What's more important, such a model can nurture our own school back. The sent-out teachers and cadres upgrade their educational experience and management skills. The way to transfer mainstay teachers and pull young teachers to step in can also facilitate a more efficient growth for talent echelon. The famous schools will not be hollowed-out at all, but become better. This is "sending other roses and leave a lingering fragrance in hands".

98. 教育帮扶需要久久为功

　　教育是成风化人的事业，需要久久为功。教育帮扶也是如此，不能只作短期计划，而要有长远谋划。只要还存在教育资源配置不均衡的现象，优质学校就有开展教育帮扶的社会责任。教育帮扶不能靠一时的激情，而需要长期的努力。教育帮扶难在坚持不懈、贵在坚持不懈，要有一张蓝图干到底、咬定青山不放松、不达目的不罢休的干劲和韧劲。只有这样，才能把教育帮扶这件惠及当代、利在千秋的大事办好。

98. Educational poverty alleviation is a long-term effort

Education is an undertaking that initiates public morals and makes positive influence on people, so it requires making a long-term efforts. So is educational poverty alleviation. We can't just make short-time plans but a long-term strategy. As long as there is an imbalanced distribution of education resources, excellent schools have the social responsibility to make contribution to educational poverty alleviation. Educational poverty alleviation can't just be a temporary passion but a long-term effort. The difficulty of it lies in persistence, and the value is also persistence. We should have the motivation and tenacity to follow the blueprint through to the end, never give up or waver and will not stop until the goal is reached. Only in such a way can we do right about educational poverty alleviation, the grand cause that fits the interests of the current and future generations.

99. 教育均衡的关键在师资

　　实现教育均衡，关键在干部、师资。当前，我们最缺乏的是具有先进教育理念的优秀校长和优秀教师，只有干部、师资水平基本达到均衡，才可能谈得上教育均衡。鉴于此，优质校在促进基础教育优质均衡发展的过程中，一方面要将自身培养的优秀人才向外输送，另一方面要努力为全国各地培训大量优秀校长和优秀教师。

99. The crucial point of education equilibrium is faculty

In order to achieve education equilibrium, the crucial point is personnel and faculty. Currently, what we lack are excellent headmasters and teachers with advanced educational concepts. Only when the basic level of personnel and faculty becomes balanced, shall we speak about education equilibrium. For that reason, in the process of facilitating the development of education equilibrium on basic education, excellent schools should: on one hand, send out remarkable talents cultivated by the schools, and on the other hand, try to train a big quantity of excellent principals and teachers for other places in our country.

100. 利用信息化手段实现优质教育资源辐射的最大化

互联网使优质教育资源能够到达世界的每一个角落，充分利用信息化手段扩大优质教育资源的覆盖面，是解决当前优质教育资源相对匮乏的一个有效途径。

100. Maximize the radiation of excellent education resources with information-based methods

The Internet allows excellent educational resources to reach every corner of the world. Taking full advantage of information-based methods to extend the coverage of excellent educational resources is an effective way to solve the problem of a lack of excellent educational resources.

视频集锦
A Collection of Videos

责任编辑：张伟珍　关　宏

装帧设计：曹　春　汪　莹

图书在版编目（CIP）数据

教书育人100句 / 刘彭芝 著 .—北京：人民出版社，2020.1（2020.9 重印）

ISBN 978 - 7 - 01 - 021291 - 3

I. ①教… II. ①刘… III. ①教育工作 - 经验 - 中国　IV. ① G52

中国版本图书馆 CIP 数据核字（2019）第 208191 号

教书育人100句

JIAOSHU YUREN 100 JU

［中英对照］

刘彭芝　著

人民出版社 出版发行

（100706　北京市东城区隆福寺街 99 号）

北京新华印刷有限公司印刷　新华书店经销

2020 年 1 月第 1 版　2020 年 9 月北京第 2 次印刷

开本：710 毫米 ×1000 毫米 1/16　印张：13.75

字数：39 千字　印数：10,001—20,000 册

ISBN 978 - 7 - 01 - 021291 - 3　定价：49.80 元

邮购地址 100706　北京市东城区隆福寺街 99 号

人民东方图书销售中心　电话（010）65250042　65289539